# Carving for Kids

Robin Edward Trudel

Linden Publishing

Fresno

Carving for Kids
by Robin Edward Trudel

ISBN-13: 978-1-933502-02-1
ISBN-10: 1-933502-02-9
Printed in China
3579864

Library of Congress cataloging-in-publication data

Trudel, Robin Edward, 1966-
  Carving for kids / Robin Edward Trudel.
     p. cm.
   ISBN-13: 978-1-933502-02-1 (pbk. : alk. paper)
   ISBN-10: 1-933502-02-9 (pbk. : alk. paper)
   1. Wood-carving.  2. Wood-carving -- Technique.  I.  Title.
TT199.7.T78 2006
736'.4--ds22

                                    2006003717

**Your safety is your responsibility.** Neither the author nor the publisher assume any responsibility for any injuries suffered or for damages or other losses incurred that may result from the material presented in this publication. Some woodworking machinery in this book may have been photographed without the guards in place. This was done for clarity only. All guards and safety equipment shuld be fully functional and properly employed in all woodworking operations at all times.

Linden Publishing Inc.
2006 S. Mary St.
Fresno, CA 93721  USA
tel 800-345-4447
www.lindenpub.com

# Contents

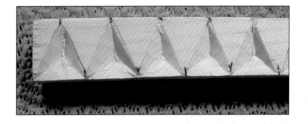

## Introduction

In today's disposable culture, the desire for learning the skills of an artisan seems to be diminishing. Why learn to carve a wooden spoon when you can buy one for a dollar? Art and shop classes are frequently early targets as educational budgets dwindle.

As I observe this phenomenon in our society, a question comes to mind: "Who will bring the joy of creation to children?"

Exposure is critical. Expose a child to woodcarving and although they may not become the next Michaelangelo, that interest may lead to a career or a lifelong interest. Interest in wood can lead a child to pursue a career as a carpenter or furniture maker. Interest in art can lead to a career as an artist, graphic designer, or even an architect. In the shorter term, teens looking for a way to express themselves may find sculpture a possible alternative to less positive choices.

People can only develop interests in things they have been exposed to. The more positive methods of self-expression a child is exposed to, the more likely they will express themselves in a positive fashion.

A simple text can't teach everything. This book is to help educate the instructor both about woodcarving and about teaching children. It also hopes to provide a resource to develop carving sessions for children and to spark the interest of people of all ages in woodcarving

Woodcarving can be an occasion for people of different generations to learn together to do something fun and productive.

You can help the child to understand that not only can they learn to shape wood, but to shape other things, including their lives.

## Things kids have taught me

Children can be amazing teachers if you give them the chance.

My wife and I have four children. Each of them is graced with dramatically different strengths and challenges.

We adults sometimes forget the value of simple things. A stick found in the yard can become Excalibur, a rifle, a tent pole, or a hundred other things. A four-year-old's favorite Christmas item may not be the expensive educational toy but the box it came in. I fondly remember a large corrugated cardboard box that my grandmother gave me. At first, it was a train. After my grandmother loaned me a magic marker I made it into a car, then a spaceship. I don't remember a lot of the store-bought toys I had at that age, but that box won't soon be forgotten.

So, why do I remember the box? Because I was invested in it. I created the box, decided what it would be and modified it as my whim changed.

When a child invests in something like a woodcarving, it becomes very personal. Helping a child to bring something into the world that did not exist before is a very powerful statement to a child. With time the child will gain more skills and confidence and want to create something entirely new. What more exciting moment than taking something that existed only in your mind's eye and producing it for the entire world to see.

Some children are more interested in completing a project than enjoying the steps of creating it, it is important for a child to understand that they can shape the world around them. Each child will put something different into and get something different out of the creative process.

It's important not to force the process, let children explore woodcarving at their own pace.

## Introduction to woodcarving

It is unfortunate that we have few examples of the woodcarvings of early man. Woodcarvings must be cared for and even then, time is not kind to them. Sculpture has always been with us. Early man had access to wood and sharp stones and combined the two to make some of the earliest tools.

Whittling usually refers to wood sculpture using one tool. Woodcarving refers to the use of several tools. Woodcarving is probably as old as tools. Early man used sharp rocks to shape spears, staffs, and other implements.

David LaHue introduced me to woodcarving. Dave had been, among other things, a carpenter and a furniture maker. We worked together for several years and he shared his love of woodworking with me. One Christmas he was kind enough to buy me a woodcarver's bench knife and a block of basswood. He gave me some basic instructions and directed me to carve a mushroom. Many chips and bandages later I had a mushroom-looking object. And I was hooked.

Then there was Mark Boulanger. Mark was a carpenter at the company where Dave and I worked. When I received a promotion I saw more of Mark and less of Dave. Mark is a talented woodworker and showed me many tricks of the trade.

I started hitting the library looking for information on U.S. carousel carvers, folk carvers, ships figureheads, and tramp carving. Most of the books from the library were from the 1940's and 1950's but one author stood out, E. J. Tangerman.

His first woodcarving book was a pamphlet for the Boy Scouts. His single-minded mission seemed to be to document all of the woodcarving knowledge he could find. His search took him to South America and the Pacific Rim as well as Europe. My first few carving years were filled with pieces I carved from patterns in his books.

Somewhere during that period I found the New England Woodcarvers. I was amazed to discover such an open-armed group of people. Two past-presidents of the organization, Rip Stangroom and M. Paul Ward were both kind enough to offer advice and helpful criticism.

As I explored my French Canadian roots I discovered the works of Jobin, Cote, Borgault, and of course Benoit Deschenes. Their figure carving appealed to me and still has an influence on my work.

Throughout my journey of looking for more about woodcarving I have been fortunate to discover people who were eager to share their learning and this is my opportunity to share my learning with you.

# Introduction to wood

A piece of wood is a section of a tree. A tree can be described as a series of concentric cones. Each year a tree grows, it is adding a new "cone." Take a section of log from the tree and split it into wedges. Pick up a wedge and split off the bark. "With the grain" is different depending on where you are in this wedge. If you're cutting into the wood from the bark side chances are (barring knots and the like) "with the grain" is cutting from the root to the top of the tree. If you're cutting into the wood from the heartwood side cutting from the top of the tree to the roots is "with the grain" usually. Not a hard and fast rule, but I have found that this description helps new carvers visualize grain structure.

## White Pine - *Pinus strobus*

By far, Eastern white pine is the wood I use the most. It is readily available all over North America. Most folks can recognize it by sight although in lumber form it is easily confused with spruce and fir which are generally not good wood carving material.

White pine can be purchased in smaller sizes and laminated, or you can look for a lumber mill in your area to get larger sizes. There is a lumber mill up the street from me where I can get 8 inch x 8 inch stock in pieces five and six feet long with ease. Large blocks can also be obtained, but they are a disappointment when they check during seasoning.

Many towns have a log graveyard where homeowners can dump logs. Since white pine is not good for use in a residential fireplace many of the logs you'll find in these graveyards are white pine. There are problems with these dumped logs. They will probably be cut carelessly and there will be knots and probably bits of old nails and screws embedded in the wood.

The pine I buy comes in three types that I call sugar, soap, and striped. Sugar is easiest to cut, but crumbles and dents easily. Soap is a little harder, white with little visible grain, and is the best for most work. The striped pine has marked stripes, but carves much like the "soap." These are just names I made up for my own reference. I suspect these types depend more on growing conditions and are not sub-species. A rule of thumb is the whiter the wood and the harder to detect the grain rings (in finished lumber) the better it will be for carving. It's just a guideline as most eastern white pine is easy to carve, sand, and stamp.

What it is not, is strong. Thin members such as cross-grained sections are doomed. Design your carving so that cross-grained sections are supported.

### Basswood - *Tilia americana*

Basswood is the most popular wood among woodcarvers. The best northern basswood is a dream to work with and the stringy southern varieties are irritating. It's not something you can find in a lumber store or at a lumber mill unless there is a large local surplus. Specialty hardwood vendors will have it in stock and it is available via mail order from many places.

Basswood is very forgiving, stains well and is easy to carve. It is very plain; the grain is not very visible which makes it excellent for painting.

### Butternut - *Juglans cinerea*

I like using butternut. It carves as easy as pine or basswood, but has a definite figure that can enhance the appeal of a carving. It too is something you will most likely have to order.

### Black Walnut - *Juglans nigra*

Black Walnut is a little more difficult to carve, but a beautiful wood. It sands well and finishes very well and is almost as easy to obtain as white pine.

### Northern White Cedar - *Thuja occidentalis*

This aromatic wood is sometimes easy to get locally. Sharp tools are a must and sanding has mixed results - raises too many fuzzies. A pleasure to work because of the smell, detailed pieces are possible, but dull tools will make you want to pull your hair out.

### Eastern Red Cedar - *Juniperus virginiana*

Red Cedar is hard to get in large pieces because it is difficult to season. A little harder than pine, the contrasting red and white can make a striking carving. Sharp tools are a must, and sanding is OK.

### Black Cherry - *Prunus serotina*

Cherry is a beautiful wood. In time some pieces age to a deep golden red color. It is difficult to stamp but sands and carves well, although with more effort than some other woods. It takes finishes well and responds to an oil finish very nicely. It's stronger than most of the other woods mentioned here which consequently makes it more difficult to shape. Highly figured cherry can be difficult to carve because the grain changes from inch to inch. Some lumber yards will mix apple in with cherry and not know the difference. In my experience apple is much more difficult to carve.

## Seasoning wood

Fresh cut timber is full of moisture. Timber cut in the winter when the sap is down will generally have less moisture. The moisture content of wood poses problems. As the moisture leaves the wood, the wood is subject to enormous stresses and cracks or checks. Controlled drying is important in minimizing this damage.

Commercial lumber is dried in a kiln. This process shortens the drying time by baking the moisture out of the wood. The process is relatively fast and efficient, but does sometimes harden the outside of the wood.

Without a kiln, the amateur must rely on air-drying. It's a less expensive process and with careful monitoring can have excellent results.

Lumber to be air-dried must be stacked so that it is protected from from the elements. Fresh green lumber needs seasoning. If you're seasoning log sections first split the log at least in half. The more splitting you do, the better for seasoning, but of course, the wood is smaller. From each of these wedges, split off the pith or the center of the tree. Remove the bark and discard it.

Moisture exits through the end grain faster than through the side grain. Painting or waxing the ends will slow down this process and decrease the chances of cracking. As the wood loses moisture it will also become lighter. The weight change can be used to determine progress.

Use thin pieces of wood to separate the individual pieces so that air can flow around them. The wood to be seasoned should be turned regularly. Airflow is rarely perfect and turning will help the wood to dry evenly and reduce stresses.

## Found wood

Wood can be found easily if you look. A short walk in the woods may yield some interesting finds. Watch out for woodborers that will ruin your piece and infest the rest of your woodpile. Ocean driftwood is surprisingly clean, but is full of abrasives that will ruin fine edges.

Pallets and leftover construction timbers are hit or miss. Many places give pallets away, but the wood is usually in miserable condition and full of embedded grit. Every once in a while though, you can find some nice pieces of cherry and once I found some mahogany.

Martial arts schools go through a surprising amount of clear wood and most of it ends up in the dumpster. I've been fortunate to be associated with a school that has supplied me with all the ¼ inch and ½ inch pine I can fit into my truck. The best time to ask is right before a rank test.

## Introduction to tools

Photo 1 - **Sanding sticks** can be made quickly and cheaply. Pictured are two types. One is a sanding fid and the other a simple sanding stick. The sanding sticks can be made with different grits of sandpaper. The sanding fid is designed so that the paper can be changed at will.

Sanding is a very safe method of shaping wood. There are no sharp edges and thus little chance of injury.

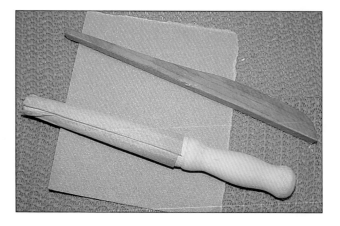

Photo 2 - **A sanding bow** can be cheaply made with a strip of abrasive belt and some scrap pine.

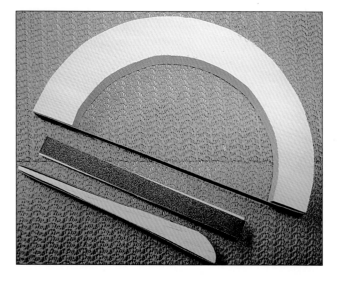

Photo 3 - **Rasps** remove a lot of wood. Microplanes(TM) are a modern update to the tried and true rasp. They are very aggressive and changing the angle of the tool can alter the coarseness of the cut. Needle files are very handy for fine work.

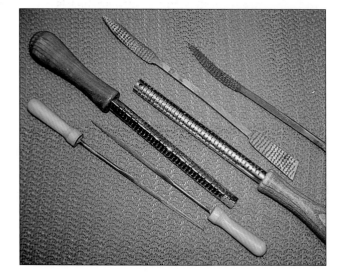

Photo 4 - Strictly speaking, **stamping** by itself is not usually considered woodcarving. However, stamping tools are a safe and effective way to introduce the youngest of children to expressing ideas in wood. Shown below are a toothed stamp, used for darkening backgrounds, and a polished point, used for lowering wood into a tight corner.

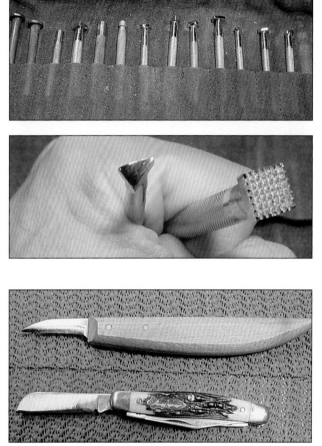

Photo 5 - **The bench knife** (top in picture) is the standard for most carvers. It has a straight carving edge and a single bevel. This single tool is enough to go from block to finished piece. The pocketknife pictured below is very portable and convenient, but while carving it is important to remember that the blade folds. If the blade were to fold while someone was carving, they could easily be cut.

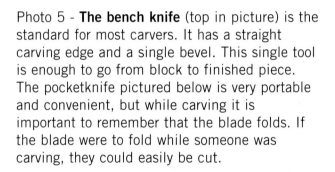

Photo 6 - **Palm tools** with mushroom heads evolved from tools that engravers used. They are excellent for light work with one hand holding the blank and the other hand driving the tool. A dozen shapes can easily be stored in a small tackle box. These tools cannot be used with a mallet.

Photo 7 - **S. J. Addis** manufactured this tool. It probably dates back to the mid to late 1800's. These tools can either be pushed with the palm or driven with a mallet. A woodcarving mallet is different than a hammer. The tapered cylindrical head of the mallet is specifically for driving woodcarving tools. The taper ensures a good striking angle. It is a cylinder so that it may strike the gouge solidly no matter which part faces forward.

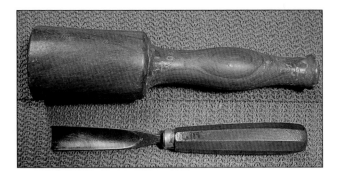

Photo 8 - Pictured here are a **sharpening stone, a strop and jeweler's rouge.** Sharpening is something that could fill several volumes by itself. The basics are this: Lubricate the stone. Lay the blade on the stone so that the bevel is flat to the stone. Rub away the metal on the blade until you have created a wire edge. Flip the knife over and do the other side.
After the wire edge is created, strop the knife on the leather strop. The jeweler's rouge should be rubbed into the leather. Stropping is done with a pulling motion, the opposite of a cutting motion. This polishes the blade further and eventually the wire edge will fall off.
Stropping should be done frequently. The blade should only be sharpened when damaged, or when stropping is no longer effective.

Photo 9 - **Sanding bows** are available commercially, but a piece of wood ¾ x 8 x 6 inches and some abrasive belt is all that is required to make one. Trace an arc from corner to corner with a compass as pictured. Trace a second arc one inch smaller and inside the first arc.

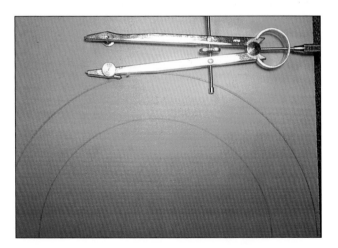

Photo 10 - **Cut the bow out** using a band saw, scroll saw or coping saw.

Photo 11 - **Use thumbtacks** to tack on ½-inch wide abrasive belts. Prepare several different grit belts to put on the bow. The sanding sticks pictured with the completed bow are the next tools to make.

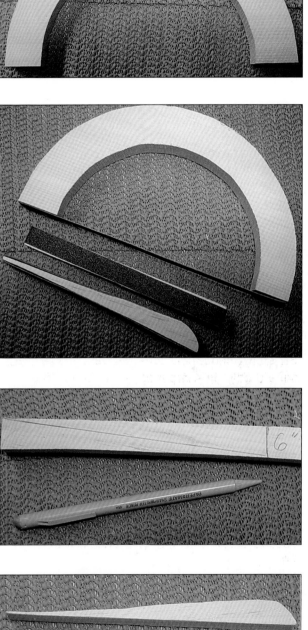

Photo 12 - **Mark off** an eight-inch length on a ¾ inch x ¾ inch stick. Draw a diagonal line from corner to corner.

Photo 13 - **Saw along the lines** to create two sanding sticks. Measure some abrasive belt by wrapping it around the whole stick. White glue can be used to hold it in place. The coarsest grit sticks will remove wood quite rapidly.

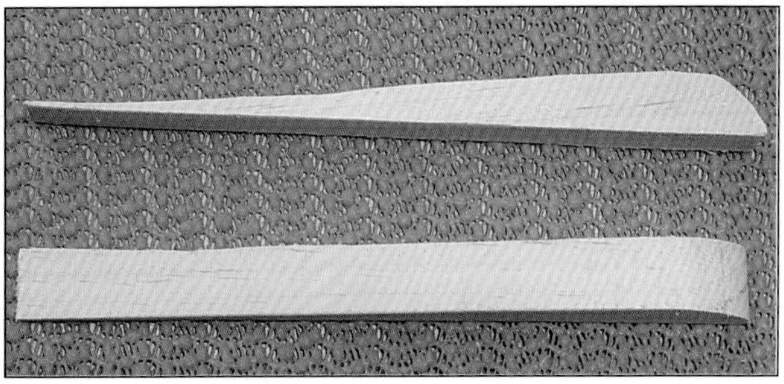

## Making the tools for the projects

Photo 14 - **This is a sanding fid** with the sandpaper removed. A dowel with a slot in it will work just fine, but I turned this one on a lathe.

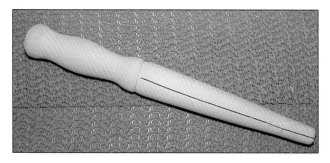

Photo 15 - **A piece of sandpaper** specially measured for the fid is cut and wrapped around the fid. The ends are tucked into the slot. It should fit very snugly. If the sanding fid is tapered, pulling the sandpaper down the fid will lock it into place by friction. The sanding bow, stick and fid combined can be a very versatile and safe toolkit.

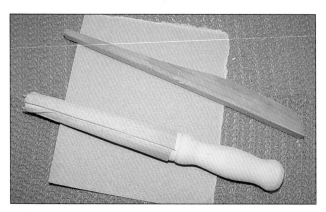

Photo 16 - **Stamping tools** are available commercially from leatherworking suppliers. On the left is a polished point. On the right is a cut steel nail that I ground and polished. When grinding the stamps to shape please be sure to frequently dip the cut nail into water to keep it cool. If you burn the steel it will become less durable.

Photo 17 - On the left is a **square polished setter**. On the right is a rough ground cut steel nail ready to be polished. It takes about 10 minutes to make a cut steel nail into a stamp. Be sure to grind the point of the nail flat.

Photo 18 - **To make a toothed stamp**, start with a large headed nail. It should be about the size of a dime. File a series of perpendicular lines. The lines should be close together and very regular. The lines pictured in this photo are a bit wide apart. The peaks of the lines should just about be touching.

Photo 19 - **Now file in** some perpendicular lines and the toothed stamp is ready.

## A brief introduction to carving

The best method for teaching this is to get sticks, or 1 x 1s, and let the students practice these cuts without a project in mind. There's way too much pressure on new students to 'finish something'. That's when the Band-Aids come in handy. To learn the basics, get a woodcarving knife and a ¾ inch x ¾ inch stick.

There are three basic cuts in whittling, the paring cut, the levering cut, and the stop cut.

Photo 20 - **The paring cut.** It's just like peeling a potato. Hold the wood with one hand, the knife in the other. Brace the thumb of the knife hand against the carving, but not where you will cut yourself when the knife slips, because it will slip. Peel off a thin slice of the wood, with the grain, by closing your hand and pulling the knife towards yourself. If you cut into the grain your knife will stick, or you will break off more than you planned.

Photo 21 - **The stop cut.** Used with either of the other cuts, this is what gets the work done. Hold the wood with one hand, the knife in the other. Brace the thumb of the knife hand against the carving. Use the tip of the knife to make a controlled slice into the wood. When you're done, you haven't removed any wood, you've just created a 'break'. Use a paring cut or levering cut to remove wood up to the stop cut.

Photo 22 - The result is a **nice clear notch** in the stick.

Photo 23 - **The levering cut.** Mom's favorite cut. Hold the wood with one hand, the knife in the other. Brace the thumb of the knife hand against the carving, but not where you will cut yourself when the knife slips, because it will slip. Peel off a thin slice of the wood, with the grain, by turning your wrist outward using your thumb as the fulcrum and the knife edge as the lever. This is the move you see in the movies where old-timers are whittling pointed sticks.

Photo 24 - **Repeat the stop cut** and a nice clear notch is the result.

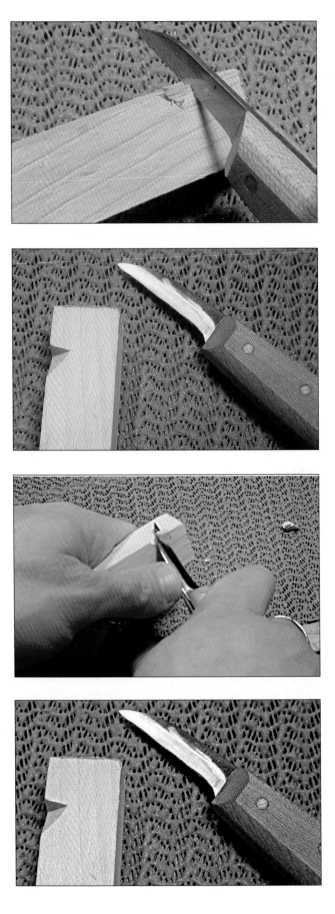

## Mushroom

My first carving was a mushroom. The mushroom is a simple and an easy way to learn about the three cuts and working with the grain. To get started cut a piece of basswood 1 inch x 1 inch and about 2 inches long.

About a ⅓ of an inch from the base, mark a line on all four sides. Carefully band saw the line in on all four sides to a depth of about ¼ inch. About a half-inch from the top, draw a line around the top of the blank. This will mark the bottom of the cap.

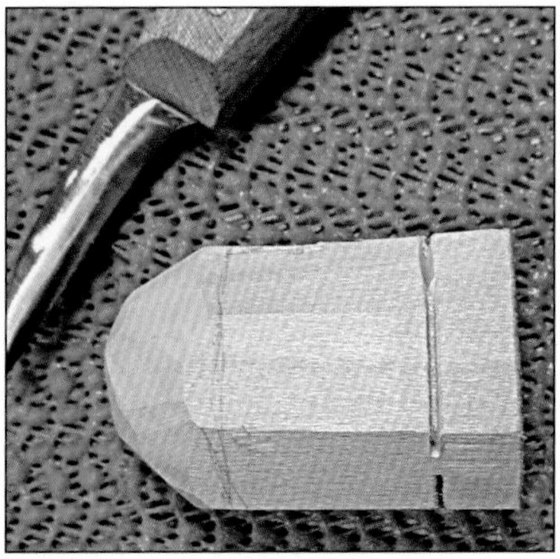

Photo 25 - **Round the top** of the cap of the mushroom using paring cuts. Don't carve below the line.

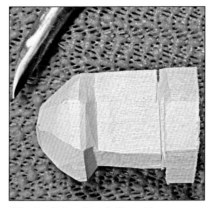

Photo 26 - **To define the cap** first make a stop cut under the cap, then pare up to it. The saw has made a stop cut for you so pare down to it.

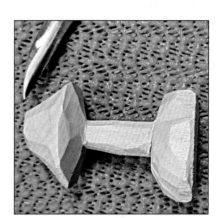

Photo 27 - **Repeat** the process until the stem is shaped. Use the knife and some paring cuts to make the base interesting.

## Egg

An egg is another simple but effective exercise. Get a piece of wood 1 inch x 1 inch and about 1 and ¾ inches long and draw an egg shape onto it. Start by paring off one of the corners. Move on to the other three corners, taking care to maintain the egg shape.

Photo 28 - **Turn the egg** on its side and redraw it.

Photo 29 - Now **carve off** these corners.

Photo 30 - All that's left to do is to **round the egg**.

# Pyramid

This last exercise will help to understand depth.

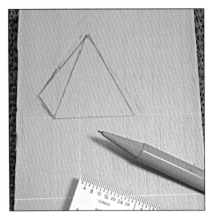

Photo 31 - Using the picture as an example, **draw a 3D pyramid** on a piece of white pine.

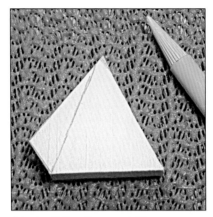

Photo 32 - **Saw out the pyramid.** To create the illusion of depth, the pyramid needs to be tapered. The bottom should be the thickest tapering to the point. Draw a reference line along the side.

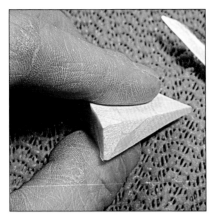

Photo 33 - **Carefully pare** down the pyramid from the base to the tip.

Photo 34- **Redraw** the angle of the partially visible face.

Photo 35 - **Carefully pare** off the wood at an angle. The grain may go in either direction so be sure to test with a smaller cut first.

Photo 36 - **The completed pyramid** should resemble the one in the photo.

## Chip carving

Chip carving is a wonderful way to decorate unfinished pine items that are readily available from craft stores. To learn these techniques, prepare a ¾ inch x ¾ inch stick with marks every ½ inch.

Photo 37 - **Mark the opposite edge** with marks in the middle of the original marks, as in the photo.

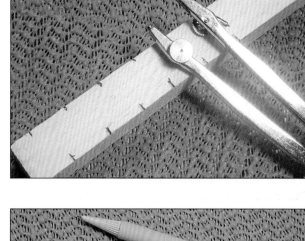

Photo 38 - **Connecting the dots** will make a series of triangles. Inside each of these triangles draw three more smaller triangles.

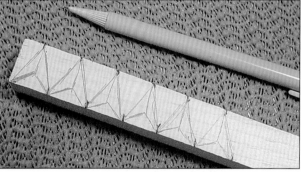

Photo 39 - **To begin carving,** insert the knife tip into the wood along one of the lines. The stop cut should be deepest in the center and shallowest at the outside.

Photo 40 - **Make the second** stop cut the same way.

Photo 41 - **Insert the knife tip** into one of the corners and pare down to the other line. The blade should be parallel with the stop cut that will finish the cut.

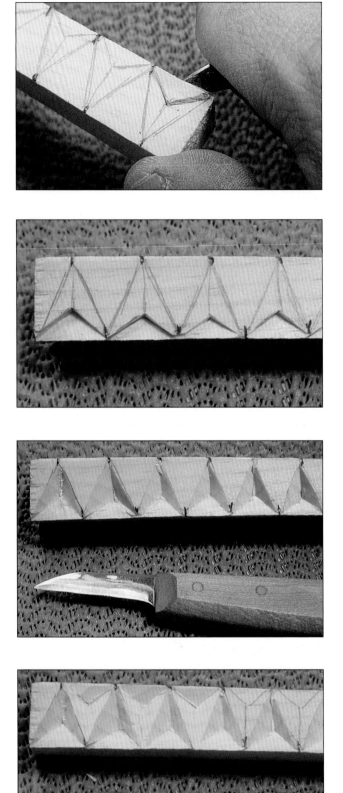

Photo 42 - **This technique** is referred to as the "three cut". Run these along the bottom of the stick.

Photo 43 - **The "six cut"** is composed of three "three cuts." Finish the six-cuts down the stick.

Photo 44 - **You can also carve** the triangles on the other side for an interesting effect.

## Preparing a project

The next three chapters deal with carving projects for children of different ages. The projects will go much easier if time is spent in preparation.

Find a project box to keep items in between sessions. Plastic boxes are fine, but I have always found cardboard soda boxes or shoeboxes with lids to be convenient. Tackle boxes come in many different sizes and work quite well.

Get all of the details ready in advance and put then in the project box. Children are less likely to lose things if they have their own case.

If you have time, any visual aids you can prepare will be helpful. Step by step models will also be very helpful. For instance, for the mushroom project prepare a partially carved mushroom for each picture. Line them up for the student to review and touch. Photos of the subject of the carving, if they are available, are also helpful.

## Woodworking and challenged kids

The U.S. Census Bureau states that 49 million Americans have some sort of physical disability. That does not take into account people who are developmentally or physically challenged.

Like any other child, challenged children want to be self-reliant. They need to be taught in a manner that maintains their dignity and boosts their self confidence. Most children are capable of producing at least one of the projects in this book. M. Paul Ward, past president of the New England Wood Carvers, has used stamping projects similar to those in this book to introduce challenged children to woodworking.

These children should not be left out because they are differently abled. I have two challenged children, two cousins, and many friends with challenged children. Consider for a moment the case of Dr. Stephen Hawking. He cannot walk or talk. He depends on help for the simplest tasks, yet his mind embraces the universe and communicates in a plain fashion that the average person can grasp. It has been theorized that Michaelangelo may have been autistic. The list of challenged, but creative, people is endless.

Can woodcarving give these children self reliance? Perhaps not, but it can be used to boost their self-confidence. It could easily be argued that if you give someone self-confidence and treat them with dignity and in the process showed them how to do something for the first time, it will contribute to their personal independence.

All children, especially challenged children, need a creative outlet. As in working with any child, try to use the child's motivations to help the project. If the child likes soccer, maybe instead of making a flower, you make a soccer ball. Teaching works best when you are helping them do something they already want to do, rather than forcing your plan upon them.

Like all children, challenged children have different learning styles. Some challenged children are brighter than most children, but have a learning style that makes knowledge acquisition difficult in our culture. If you can find a way to teach such a child, the possibilities are endless. Some children suffer from challenges that will require you to build shortcuts into the project. Don't be afraid to do this, but modify the project in such a way that you maintain the child's dignity.

# Chapter One: The Youngest (ages 4 to 8)

One Sunday afternoon my youngest boy Marc and I were in the supermarket. He was about six at the time and he spotted a package of cookie dough in the refrigerated case. He made his best puppy dog face and asked if I would buy the cookie dough and make him some cookies.

"Sure, I'll buy them but you'll make them."

"But I'm just a kid!"

"If you want them, you have to make them."

He was pretty skeptical but after shopping we went back to the house and made the cookies. The process was pretty simple, open the package, put the dough balls on the sheet and place the sheet in the oven. But that wasn't the point. At the end of a half-hour, he had baked cookies. A task he thought impossible. Cookies come from a package, not from little boys.

Later that night when other members of the family returned home he met them at the door with one of "his cookies." That event, that opening of the child's world to the possibility that something that exists only in their mind can be brought into reality is very powerful. Vision is humanity's strongest tool. The pyramids began as an idea in one man's head.

For this group of projects I kept in mind a few basic principles. First, the project had to be achievable in one sitting. If I had tried to keep Marc's focus through sifting flour, cracking eggs, mixing dough, adding chocolate and so on it's likely that I would have lost his attention and ended up making the cookies myself.

The projects should be personal. Children's names have special power at the age when they are just learning to read and write. Marking their name on paper is a big step; capturing it in a carving creates something even more tangible.

## Teaching kids of this age

Children between 4 and 8 years of age are an interesting teaching challenge. Their small hands and developing motor skills mean that edged tools are out. They will be impatient and easily distracted. I've found that 20 minutes is the upper limit of their focus so plan accordingly.

Sometimes older peer modeling can help. Enlist an older child and show both children the technique. The younger child can model the older child's behavior. Of course sometimes the older child may just prove to be another distraction.

## Learning styles and techniques

Children learn differently. Be prepared to try different techniques.

There is much documentation about learning styles, but for the purposes of this book, I will discuss four types:

Children who learn by doing.

Children who learn by modeling another person's behavior.

Children who learn by seeing.

Children who learn by listening.

Some children will clearly have one style. Other children will be tough to uncover, or they may be in the process of developing a style. For a child who learns by doing it's probably best to just jump into the project. A child that relies on modeling other's behavior might benefit from watching you work on your own copy. For children that learn visually or by listening it might be a good idea to sit with them and read through the instructions before beginning.

## Levels of safety and supervision

Younger children from 4 to 6 years old need to be in an environment with fewer distractions and will need more supervision. The instructor may need to put their hands over the child's hands to help direct the work. Some 7 and 8 year olds can accept more direction and need a little less supervision.

There should be one student per instructor. Children this age will respond better to one-on-one attention.

Safety goggles are a must where a hammer is concerned. To hold the work in place, purchase a roll of non-skid material that is commonly sold as shelf lining material.

## Tools

The tools for a project of this type are very basic: a plastic mallet, and some leatherworking stamps. The crosshatch stamp and the smooth stamp are really all you need. A quick substitute for the leatherworking stamps are some cut-steel nails. Some careful work with a triangular file will create teeth every bit as good as the commercial versions. To create the smooth stamp, polish the end of another nail, relieving the corners just a bit.

Eastern white pine is a good wood to start with.

Polished "setter"

Polished pointed "setter"

Toothed stamp

Flat screwdriver

Philips screwdriver

## Workplace accommodations

The workshop might not be the best place for this age group. These projects don't make much mess and could be done almost anywhere there is a table and a chair of the correct height.

If the workshop is a must, ensure that all power tools are turned off and unplugged and that hand tools out of reach and out of sight.

## Project One: Nameplate

A child's name is very powerful. It is among the first words they learn to speak. It is usually the first word they learn to read and write.

Prepare a 3 inch x 8 inch x ½ inch board. The board should be planed or sanded smooth. The corners could also be sanded off, or perhaps rout the edge of the wood, but this is not strictly necessary. Be sure to drill a 1/2 inch hole in the back for hanging.

Ask the child to print their name carefully in big letters on the board. Don't be too concerned with the perfection of the letters, or even if the case is mixed. The idea is to capture the child's name in the child's handwriting at a moment in time.

If the child's name is too long, you might try using a nickname or perhaps their surname.

Photo 45 - **Give the child** a large flat-head screwdriver. Help the child to place the screwdriver along the lines and tap them about a millimeter into the wood. The child will want to drive it much deeper, but the final product will look much better if the lines can be kept to that depth.

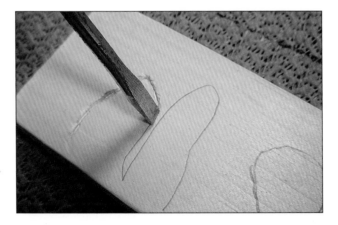

Photo 46 - **When completed**, the letters should all be stamped to a uniform depth. To protect the piece, a matte or satin polyurethane can be used. For stamped projects do not use water-based finishes. They will swell the wood and blur, or in some cases obliterate, the work.

## Project Two: Hand

Prepare an 8 inch x 8 inch x ½ inch board for this project. It should be sanded smooth and if desired a decorative edge could be routed. Before the stamping begins, drill a ½ inch hole in the back of the board for hanging.

Photo 47 - **Lay the child's hand** on the wood and trace. Keep the pencil vertical to make a consistent outline of the hand. Children tend to change the angle of the pencil to the object being traced and this creates an irregular outline. Trace lightly as these lines will be erased later.

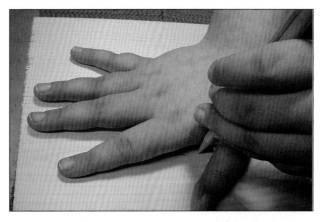

Photo 48 - **The smooth stamp** is used to stamp down the background. Place the stamp flat against the outline of the hand. Some children will not tap firmly enough to reach the correct depth with one tap. Multiple taps are fine. Consistency of the depth of the stamps is important. Help the child move and reposition the stamp. Each move forward should slightly overlap the previous stamp mark. The most difficult spots will be between the fingers.

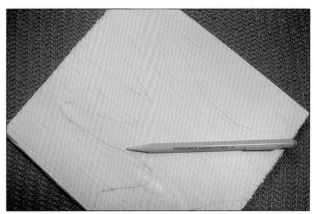

Photo 49 - **Once the outline** is completely stamped, switch to the toothed stamp. This stamp will be used to darken the background. The large open areas will be easiest for most children. The way to ensure a consistent looking background is to stamp, then move the stamp half its width and turn it a quarter turn and stamp again. The area between the fingers will again require careful work.

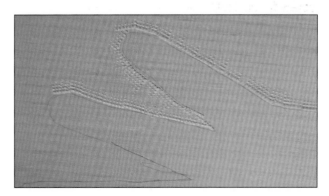

Photo 50 - **Finishing** is best done with two coats of matte or satin polyurethane. Be sure to erase the pencil lines before you apply a finish.

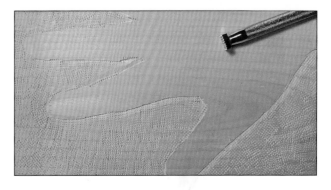

## Project Three: Name sculpture

Prepare an 8 inch x 8 inch x ½ inch board for this project. Don't bother to add any ornament, as this board will be sawn. Write the child's name in balloon letters. Plan carefully so that the letters are well connected.

To cut the outline use a scroll saw or a band saw with a very fine blade. For Marc's name I used a ½ inch drill to remove the center of the "a" and the "c". With the sawing complete, drill a hole in the back for hanging.

Photo 51 - **Sand the outline smooth** before beginning.
Redraw each letter onto the blank. The outside of the redrawn letters should be about ¼ inch from the edge.

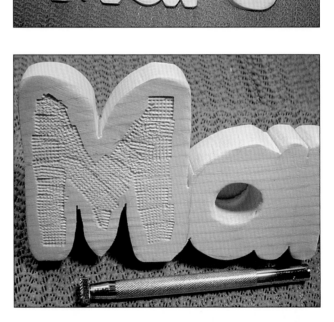

Photo 52 - **Use the toothed stamp** here to darken the letter drawn inside the sawn letters. The child should use the same turning and moving technique as earlier; stamp, move half a stamp away, quarter turn, stamp again. This work will require more attention and patience than the earlier projects.

Photo 53 - **When the stamping is complete**, it should resemble the work in the photo.
The stamps need to be firm. The completed project was finished with boiled linseed oil. Caution must be taken with the rags used, as the dryers in boiled linseed oil can produce spontaneous combustion.

## Project Four:
## Stamped Flower

Photo 54 - **The fourth project** is a little more complex. A 3 inch x 4 inch x ¼ inch piece of wood may be prepared, or as in the photo, a small basswood plaque may be purchased. These small plaques are available from many craft stores. Be sure to drill the hole in the back for hanging before any other work is done. On this plaque, draw a simple flower as shown.

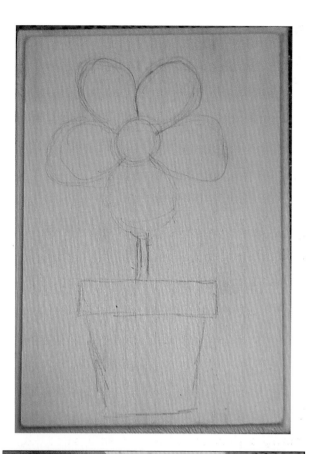

Photo 55 - **Take the pointed smooth stamp.** Help the child put the point in between the petals. A firm rap will stamp a separation between the petals.

Photo 56 - **Using the square, smooth stamp,** help the child set it on the outline of the petals. The motion here is stamp, move along half of the width of the stamp and stamp again. Work carefully in between the petals.

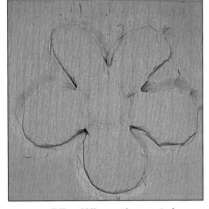

Photo 57 - **When the petals** are all stamped the project should resemble the photo.

Photo 58 - **The child can use** the Phillips screwdriver to stamp cross shapes into the center of the flower. Use care not to stamp too deeply and tear the wood fibers.

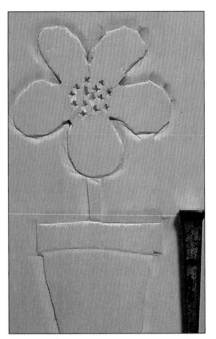

Photo 59 - **Switch back** to the flat, square, stamp and direct the child to stamp the stem and the pot. As described earlier, stamp, move half a stamp away and stamp again.

Photo 60 - **To complete the carving,** get the toothed stamp and darken the background. The technique to use for a consistent background is to stamp, move half a stamp, turn and stamp again. It's not necessary to be very precise, but it is important to cover the background evenly.

To finish this carving, linseed oil or polyurethane would do fine. A light stain before finishing would emphasize the stamped marks.

# Chapter 2: Preteens (ages 9 to 12)

I've taught several groups of young children in this age bracket. The two occasions I have in mind were organized by the 4H group here in town.

To prepare for the class I selected a project that I thought could be completed in 20 minutes or less. Having four kids of my own, I've discovered that 20 minutes is about the maximum amount of time a child can be patient. When we go to a restaurant with the whole gang and the wait is longer than 20 minutes, it's time to head back to the car and grab burgers.

For the first class I selected a whittled toy that goes by various names. It's a 6 inch or 8 inch length of dowel with a little propeller loosely nailed to the end. Notches are cut along the stick and when another stick is rubbed quickly along the notches the propeller turns.

Once I had my idea, I started making kits. First I cut the propellers out of basswood and then I trimmed some dowels to the right length. I then made some sanding sticks. There are several handy shapes you can make but for this simple project a Popsicle stick with coarse wet-dry sandpaper was enough. I made saw kerfs in the dowels and my plan was that the students would sand the saw kerfs into notches, shape the propeller a little bit and then nail the two pieces together and have fun.

I made a mistake in choosing jelutong as the dowel stock. Pine would have been almost as cheap and the sanding sticks would have made the notches much more quickly.

The children got a little frustrated sanding in the notches, but things picked up when it was time to assemble the toy and play with it.

## Teaching kids of this age

Kids between these ages are quite on their way to becoming young adults. They will certainly keep you thinking. For some kids of this age, the projects may be too much and for others they may be too simple.

Be flexible. Pay attention to the students and be prepared to regroup.

## Learning styles and techniques

For children who are visual learners, previewing the material in this section may be helpful. It might also be useful to have the book handy for the child to see the progression of photos.

Children who learn best by doing may not understand the process until they actually start carving. They will learn best by experimentation and it will probably be necessary to give these children a little more freedom to innovate.

Working with more than one child is certainly permissible. You can also make a kit for the instructor to work alongside the student and provide a model for them to emulate.

## Levels of safety and supervision

The projects in this chapter use some safe tools. As many as three or four students can be led by a single instructor.

The workshop is one place for these projects. Sanding generates a great deal of dust and that will need to be dealt with. Weather permitting, this project could be done outdoors where Nature will take care of the dust. Failing that, dust masks, appropriate ventilation and dust collection should be used. Be sure that all power tools are turned off and unplugged while the children are present.

Some people occasionally develop allergies to wood dust. Very few people are sensitive to pine and basswood, but cherry, walnut and other woods can give some people rashes. I myself have difficulty with red oak.

## Tools

Any abrasive wood tool will help shape the projects in this chapter. The sanding sticks and sanding bow described earlier will be used for these projects. A dust mask is a good addition to the project kit as well.

## Workplace accommodations

Make sure the workplace is comfortable, well lit and well ventilated. This is an ideal project to take outdoors.

## Project One: Ladybug

Photo 61 - **Kids and bugs** seem to go together. I selected a piece of red cedar about 3 inches x 4 inches x 1 inch. The child should be capable of drawing the beetle on the blank.
First draw an oval that fills one side of the block. Next, bisect the oval with a line. At one end make a curve for the head. At the other end, erase a bit of the line and bisect it as shown in the photo.

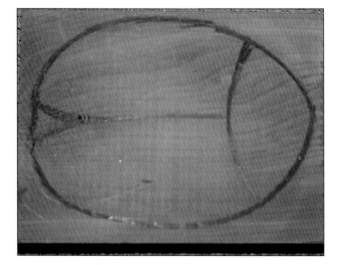

Photo 62 - **Using a band saw**, scroll saw or coping saw, cut the outline of the oval for the child.

Photo 63 - **With a pencil**, mark holes for three legs on each side.

Photo 64 - **You will need to drill** three holes. I'm fortunate to have a drill press, but the holes can be drilled with a hand-held power drill. Although the clamps are removed for the sake of the picture; the blank must be firmly clamped before drilling.

Photo 65 - **Line up all the materials** to make a kit for the child. A sanding bow, a sanding stick, three pipe cleaners cut in half to make six leg segments, and two jiggly eyes.

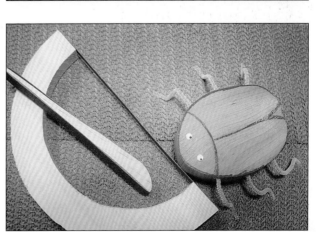

Photo 66 - **The child should trace** around the outside of the blank ¼ inch from the top. The child should then draw an oval on the top of the blank ¼ inch away from the edge of the top. When complete, the blank should be marked similar to the photograph. The portion marked off needs to be removed. The child could use either the sanding stick or bow.

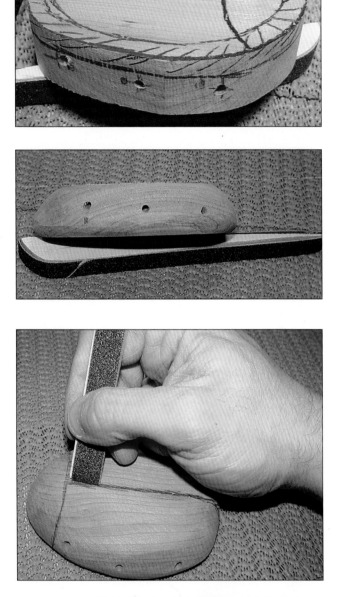

Photo 67 - **With the corners** sanded off, the next step is to round the rest of the blank.

Photo 68 - **You or the child** should next re-draw the lines onto the wood. Holding the sanding stick as a pencil, the child should sand in the lines with a scrubbing motion.

Photo 69 - **Using the sanding stick**, lower the face side of the line that defines the head. The wings should be at one level and the head about ¹⁄₁₆ inch lower.

Photo 70 - **The jiggle eyes** can be glued onto the blank, added with a permanent marker, or in this case, burned in with a wood burner. First pencil in the face and then use the burning tool to set it in.

Photo 71 - **Some girls are fond** of ladybugs. To make this bug a ladybug, add three spots to each wing. For a boy, fine lines can be drawn from the head to the end of the wings.

Photo 72 - **Before adding the legs**, finish the carving with oil or polyurethane. When the finish is dry, shape and add the legs. A spot of wood glue or hot glue will hold the legs in place.

## Project Two: Barette

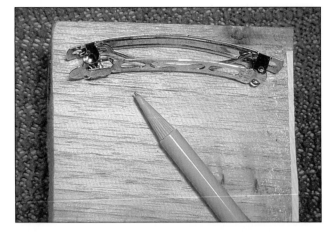

Photo 73 - **Barrette findings** can be purchased at many craft stores. If you cannot locate them, consider purchasing an inexpensive barrette and removing the finding. Select a piece of wood that will accommodate the curve of the finding. Butternut is pictured.

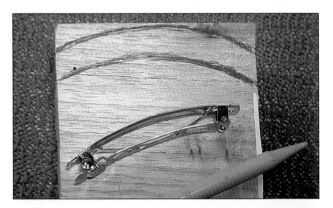

Photo 74 - **Trace the top and bottom** of the barrette onto the wood. The clasp of the finding will obstruct the tracing. After tracing, remove the barrette and clean up the lines. A good match to the curve of the finding is important.

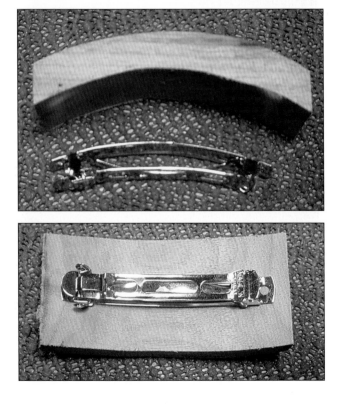

Photo 75 - **Take the block** to the band saw and cut the top and bottom. A scroll saw or coping saw will also remove the wood, but will require more effort.

Photo 76 - **Before shaping** the barrette, the slot for the finding must be carved.

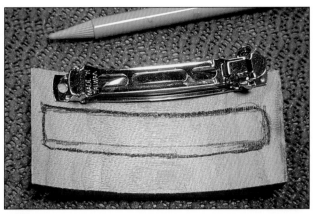

Photo 77 - **Trace the finding** on the underside of the barrette.

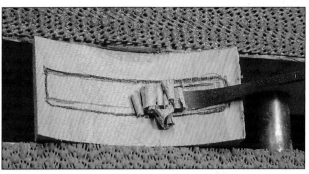

Photo 78 - **The blank must be clamped** during this next step. Trying to hold the piece of wood by hand is dangerous. Use a ½ inch chisel to carve a spot for the finding.

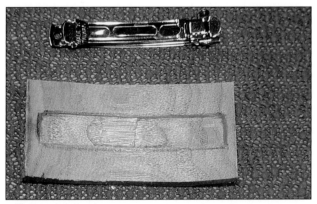

Photo 79 - **The finding** must be set with epoxy, but not until the carving is complete.

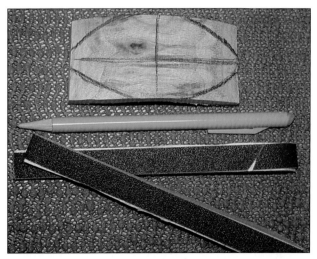

Photo 80 - **Line up the tools.** The sanding stick will do most of the work. With the pencil, draw an oval as large as possible on the top of the barrette. Sand off the corners. This will take quite a bit of work. Depending on the patience of the child, you may consider sawing this waste.

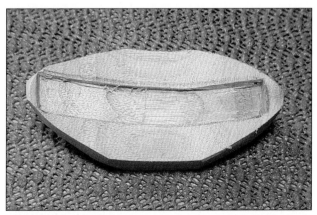

Photo 81 - **With all four corners** removed, the work on the top surface can begin.

Photo 82 - **Draw two center lines**, as pictured. Sand down the sharp edges of the top of the barrette.

Photo 83 - **Sand the whole piece** until there is one smooth unbroken surface. After the shaping is complete, take fine sandpaper and smooth the entire piece.
Two part epoxies are available from large department and hardware stores. Mix the epoxy thoroughly. An amount about the size of a half-dollar should be enough. Fill the slot with epoxy.

Photo 84 - **Press the finding** into the slot making sure that the epoxy is forced up into the holes in the finding. Leave the finding open as it dries so that the finding does not become glued shut.
Polyurethane is the best finish here. Spray several coats of a satin or matte finish.

Photo 85 - **The finished barrette**

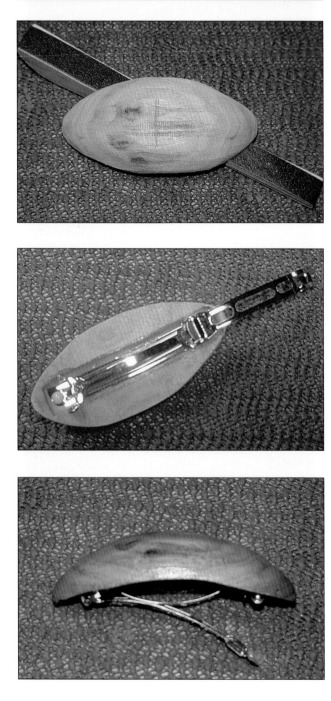

## Project 3: Spoon

Photo 86 - **This project is a little more complex.** The child should be invited to participate in the design. Cherry is a good selection. It's a tough wood and very appealing. Start with a spoon from the kitchen. Trace the bowl of the spoon onto the wood. Use a ruler to extend the shaft of the spoon about 2 inches.

Photo 87 - **A heart** is a simple design to add to the spoon. It can be traced or drawn freehand.

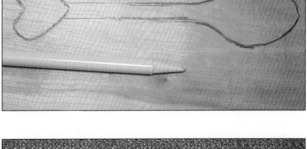

Photo 88 - **The blank** can be cut out on the band saw, a scroll saw, or a coping saw.

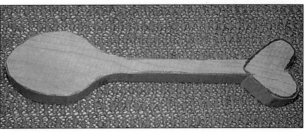

Photo 89 - **The profile** of the completed spoon should be drawn on both sides.

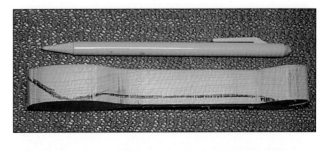

Photo 90 - **The sanding stick** can be used to round the front and back of the bowl as well as to thin the shaft. Careful work on the band saw could also remove this wood but is not recommended.

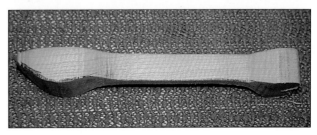

Photo 91 - **Draw an oval** on the bowl of the spoon as pictured.

Photo 92 - **Use the large rounded end** of the sanding stick to carve the bowl. This will be slow work.

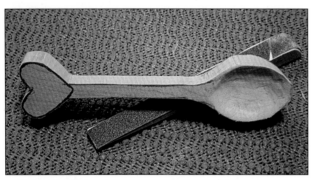

Photo 93 - **The result** of a lot of work.

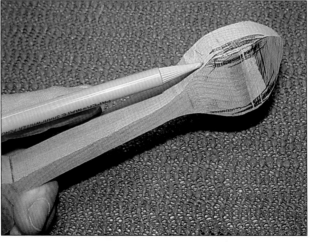

Photo 94 - **With a pencil,** mark the sides of the back of the bowl to be removed.

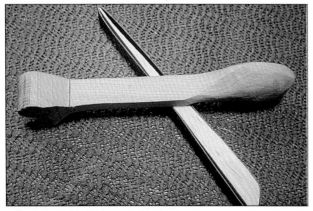

Photo 95 - **After the corners** are sanded off, smooth the entire back of the bowl. Begin shaping the heart by sanding the two rounded tops of the heart.

Photo 96 - **The tops of the heart** on one side are complete. Next, shape the bottom of the heart. Take care not to thin the handle.

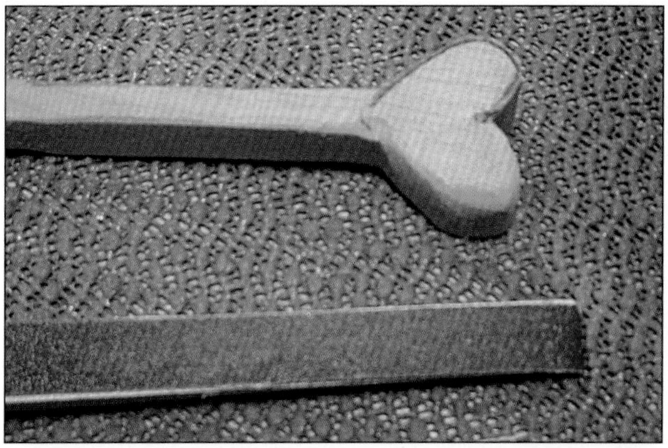

Photo 97 - **Sand the front** of the heart and down the top of the shaft on both sides. Don't forget to sand the back of the heart.

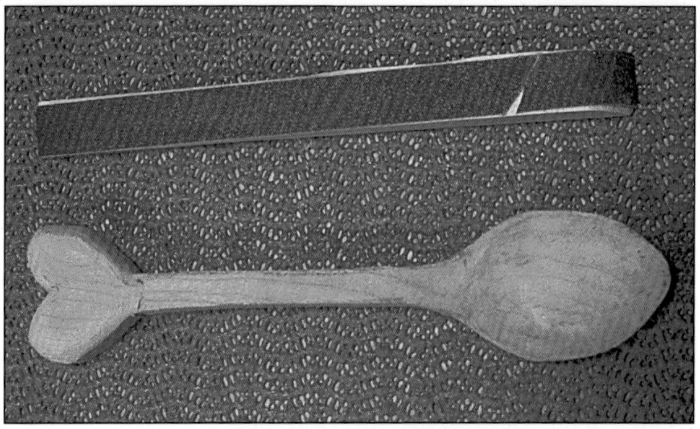

Photo 98 - **The simplest method** of smoothing the shaft of the spoon is with the bow sander. Use long strokes across the whole shaft. Turn it frequently to shape it evenly.

Photo 99 - **If the spoon** is to be used for eating, it must be finished with a non-toxic finish. Olive oil is usually safe, but the spoon will need to be re-oiled from time to time.

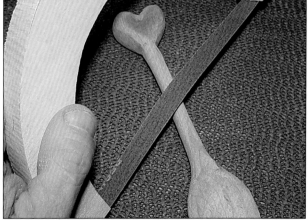

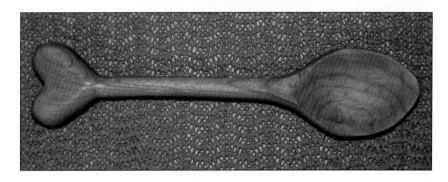

## Project Four: Snowman

Photo 100 - **Start with** a ½ inch x ½ inch x 6½ inch piece of pine or basswood. Place a mark 1 inch down the stick on all four sides. This is where the hat will meet the brim. Make another mark 1¼ inches down the stick for the bottom of the brim. Make another mark 2 inches from the end of the stick for the bottom of the face and top of the scarf. The last mark is at 2¼ inches, the bottom of the scarf.

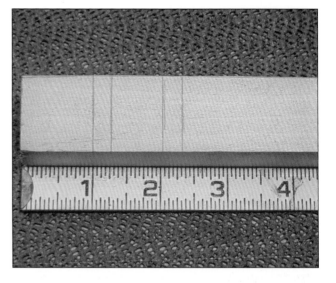

Photo 101 - **Mark a taper** on all four sides as shown in the picture.

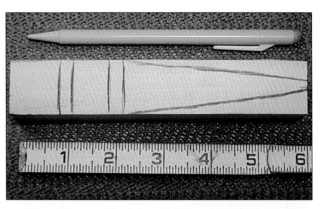

Photo 102 - **Sand or cut off** the marked taper.

Photo 103 - **Begin the hat** by sanding above the first line marked on the blank.

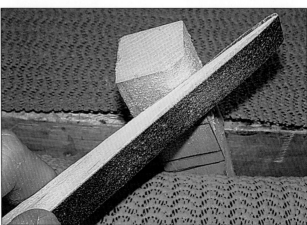

Photo 104 - **The photo represents** what one of the corners should look like.

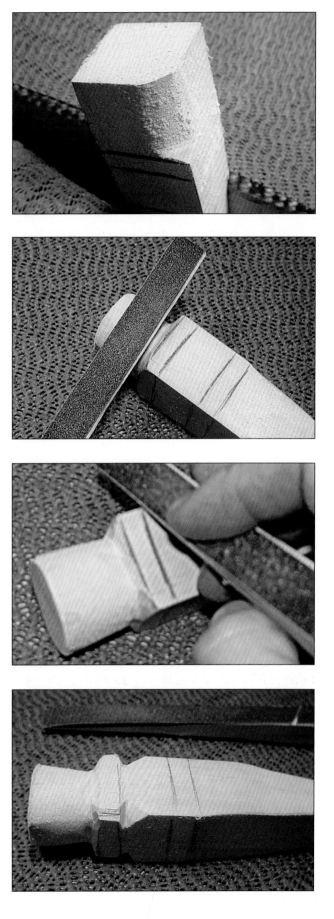

Photo 105 - **Continue to sand** off all four corners until the head is nicely rounded. Now that the hat is shaped you can begin on the brim.

Photo 106 - **Starting at the corner** begin sanding under the brim.

Photo 107 - **Connect the corners** by sanding.

Photo 108 - **Repeat the process** above the scarf.

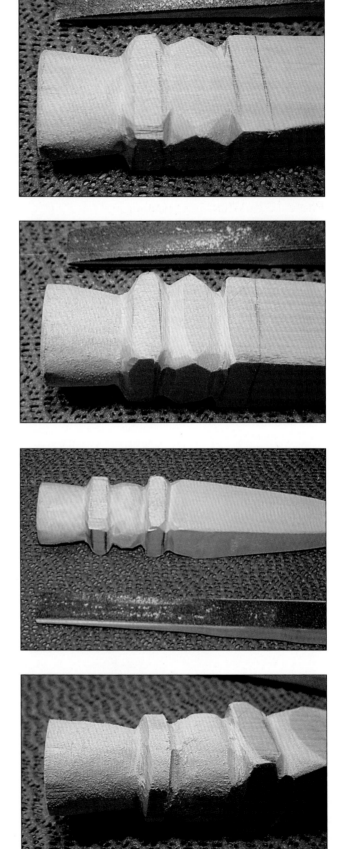

Photo 109 - **Again connect** the corners.

Photo 110 - **Connect the corners** and sand under the scarf.

Photo 111 - **Round the face first.** The sanding bow may work a little better for this work. If too much pressure is placed on the sanding stick, flat spots will be visible.

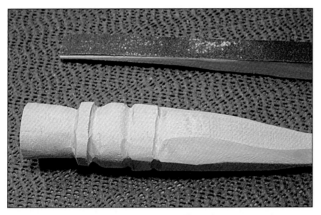

Photo 112 - **When the rounding** is done, the head, hat, and scarf should look like this photo.

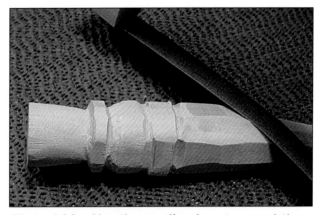

Photo 113 - **Use the sanding bow** to round the body. Long strokes at an angle will work best.

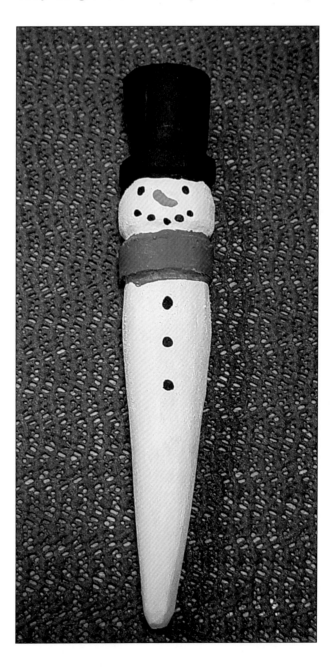

Photo 114 - **Paint the snowman** with acrylics. Black for the hat and coals, orange for the carrot and any bright color for the scarf.

# Chapter 3: Teens (ages 13 to 17)

My favorite Samuel Clemens quote:

"When I was a boy of fourteen, my father was so ignorant I could hardly stand to have the old man around. But when I got to be twenty-one, I was astonished at how much the old man had learned in seven years."

Anyone reading this book already knows how critical this time is in a young person's life. From one day to the next, it's tough to understand where the child is coming from. Stuck between being a child and a young adult, the desire to express themselves can be overwhelming. A child can only express themselves in methods they have been exposed to. Some children wrap themselves in music or friends, but some choose a more destructive path.

Can teaching a child carving save them from that more destructive path? Perhaps not. What it can do is set an example. The example that an adult is invested in their future enough to spend time with them. It can show them a way to express themselves by creating instead of destroying. Children this age should be exposed to many different methods of expression.

A few years ago, in the town where I worked, three children of this age were charged with vandalizing religious statuary on the grounds of a church. I am convinced that if someone had showed these children the effort it took to replace those statues, the world might be a better place.

## Teaching kids of this age

At this age, the child's learning style is probably set. They are developing lifetime interests and their interest in creating is much more than just "look mommy." These children can get self-satisfaction from their own work.

It is time to introduce edged tools. These children are mature enough to tackle a project that takes more than one sitting. Depending on the maturity level of the child, once they learn the basics, you may be able to let them work independently.

Have the child review the instructions, but make room for independent discovery.

## Learning styles and techniques

At this age level, every child should give the steps at least a look through. The child may even be aware of their learning style, but that's not always the case. Some children may want to pursue the project entirely on their own. I would discourage this until the child has demonstrated safe carving skills when supervised.

Children at this age will very much benefit from doing the project along with the instructor. If the child is struggling, you can trade blanks with them from time to time, "just to get them caught up." Some children will not want this sort of help and will insist on doing the work themselves.

One thing that is critically important is that if the student is being careless or is clearly not paying attention, it may be time to pack up for the day. Do not allow the student to be careless under any circumstances.

## Levels of safety and supervision

Before the children can start on the project, they need to learn the care and feeding of a knife. The carving knife will likely be the sharpest object they've ever picked up and at first they will be using it with uncertainty.

A dull knife is not a safe knife. To carve wood with a dull knife requires more force. The knife will slip and the results could be tragic.

A carving glove for the hand that holds the wood is a must. You can save a couple of dollars and use a fisherman's filet glove, but a carving glove is much better.

Make sure the child knows to strop the knife frequently. If the instructor is a confident sharpener; it will be an invaluable skill to pass on.

One last word on safety. The knife will slip. It's inevitable, especially for new carvers. The key to remaining uninjured is first, wearing a carving glove and second, hand placement.

Knowing where your hands are at all times and planning for a slip will decrease the chances for injury. When a paring cut is made, see that the thumb is below and out of the range of the blade. When doing a levering cut be sure that the holding hand is out of the way of the blade.

## Tools

All of the projects in this chapter can be completed with just a bench knife or a pocketknife with the correct blade. A ⅜-inch v-tool will help but is not required.

## Workplace accommodations

Although the children at the younger age of this group may need some height adjustments to reach the bench, generally they will be able to handle the tools. Depending on the maturity level of the children, you may decide to let them cut out their own blanks. Helping in the production of the project will give the child a peek into the entire process and perhaps their first introduction to power tools.

# Project One: Curious Duck

Photo 115 - **This duck is modeled** after a common Quebecois folk carving called "le canard curieux," the curious duck. The duck sits on the edge of a shelf and peers over. I made the sketch from memory.

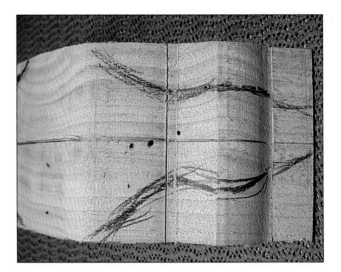

Photo 116 - **Weeping willow** is a nice hardwood to carve, but is not generally available commercially. If it is available, it is almost never available in carving block sizes. Several winters ago an ice storm took its toll on many trees and I did a neighbor a favor by dragging away this wood. I seasoned it carefully and now have a small supply of nice carving blocks. This piece is 4 inches x 4 inches x 10 inches. Select a piece of pine, basswood or butternut and trace the pattern onto your blank.

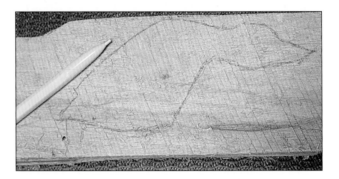

Photo 117- **Band saw the blank**. A scroll saw or coping saw would be impractical. Make sure the grain is going lengthwise as pictured here.

Photo 118 - **Draw a centerline** around the blank. The centerline will be the highest point on the blank. The line should remain uncarved until the carving is nearly complete.

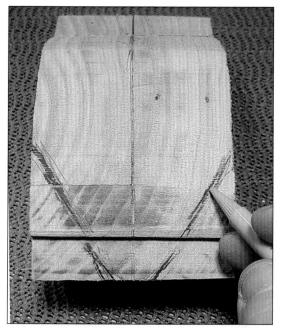

Photo 119 - **Draw the taper** for the tail as in the photo.

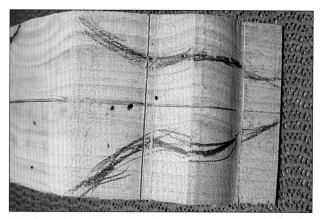

Photo 120 - **Draw the shoulder**, neck, and beak

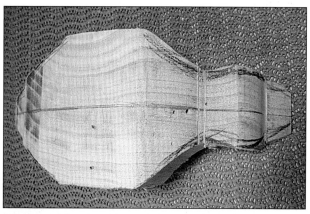

Photo 121 - **At this point** decide to if you want to band saw the pictured profile or have the student carve the waste.

Photo 122 - **This is what** the band-sawn blank should look like. If the choice is to carve off the waste it should still resemble the photo.

Photo 123 - **Draw a line** about ¼ inch to ⅜ inch off the edge of each side of the blank. The wood between these lines should be the first to be carved away.

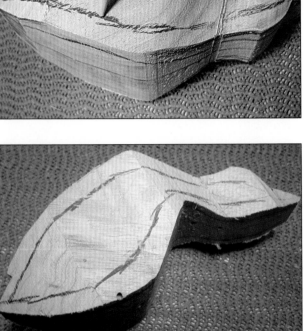

Photo 124 - **An example** of what one side of the blank should look like after it is marked off.

Photo 125 - **The paring cut** will be the cut most used on this carving. A rule of thumb is to pare from the high spots on the carving to the lower areas.

Photo 126 - **The grain changes direction** at low places like the neck. To address this, first make a stop cut.

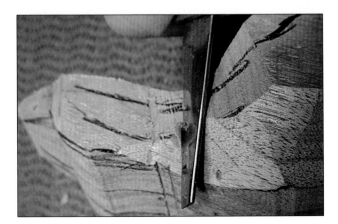

Photo 127 - **A paring cut** from the other side will trim the neck. It may take several cuts to trim the neck.

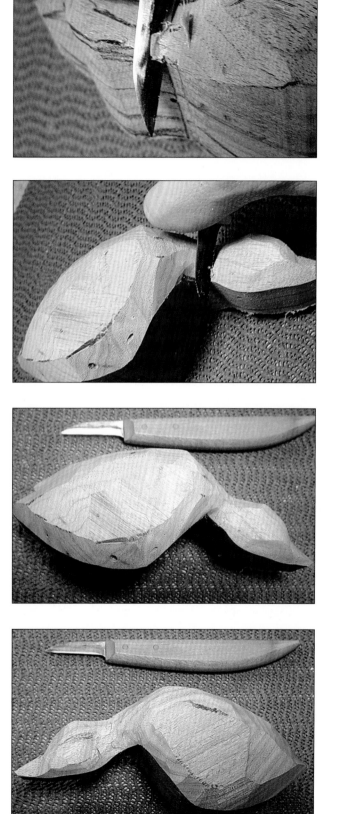

Photo 128 - **As you carve up the neck** to the head the grain will probably change directions again. As the contour of the blank changes, try a gentle cut to see if the grain has changed. If it has, cut in the other direction.

Photo 129 - **The right side** of the blank should resemble the one pictured. Once the right side is roughed in, rough in the left side. The paring cut will be used frequently. On this side of the neck levering cuts will lift up some wood. Meet those cuts with paring cuts. Continue around the left side of the duck just as before.

Photo 130 - **Both sides** are roughed in.

Photo 131 - **Start rounding the body** of the duck by paring off the sharp angle created by the roughing process.

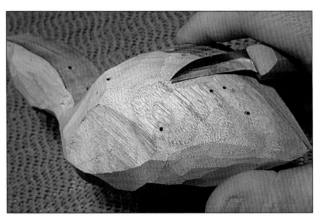

Photo 132 - **When the side of the belly** is rounded is should resemble the duck in this photo. Round the other side of the belly using the same technique. Turn the duck over and pare the angles off the back.

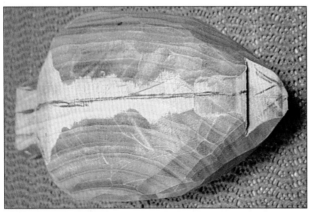

Photo 133 - **Don't forget to leave** the centerline intact. This will keep the profile of the duck intact.

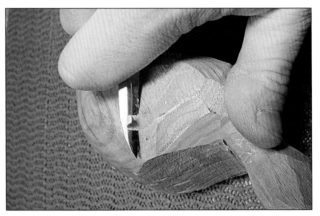

Photo 134 - **Start paring the belly** towards the flat. Be sure to leave the flat spot absolutely flat so that the duck doesn't wobble when completed.

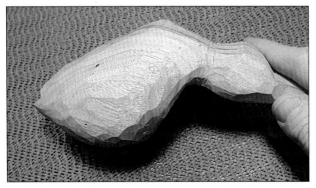

Photo 135- **Most of the rounding** is complete in this photo. Refine the neck with alternating paring and levering cuts.

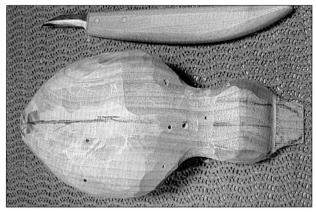

Photo 136 - **The body and neck** rounded off.

Photo 137 - **Re-draw the wings** onto the back of the duck.

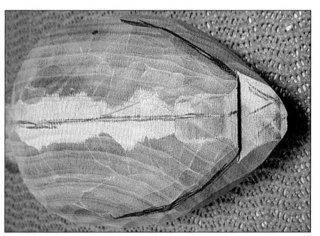

Photo 138 - **A v-tool** will make the work go easier, but a knife will also work.

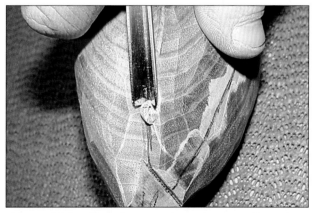

Photo 139 - **Use the v-tool** to separate the wing from the body by carving towards the tail.

Photo 140 - **Pare off the sharp angle** on the body side of the cut. Leave the sharp angle on the wing side untouched so that it creates a shadow.

Photo 141 - This is what **the wing** should look like.

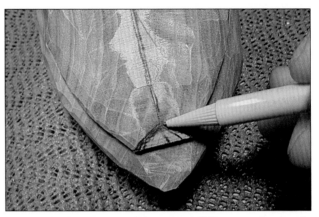

Photo 142 - **Draw an inverted "V"** onto the back of the wings.

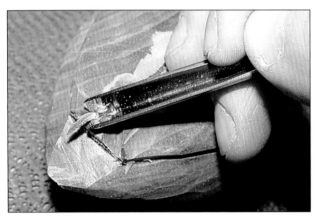

Photo 143 - **Use the v-tool**, or the knife, to set in the lines of the inverted "V."

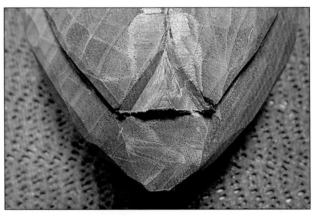

Photo 144 - **After the two cuts**, the tail should look like this.

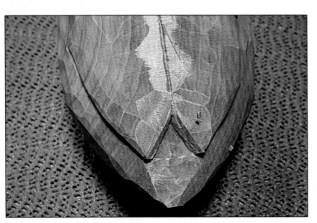

Photo 145 - **Use a levering cut** to remove the waste wood from between the wingtips. When separated the wings will resemble the photo.

Photo 146 - **Round the duck's skull** with paring cuts. Next proceed to the sides of the skull, and finally underneath the head and the bill, and the top of the head.

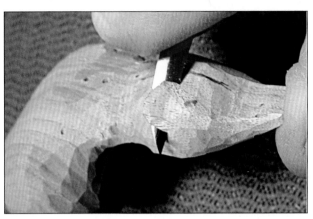

Photo 147 - **Lightly mark spots** for both eyes. Make a single, careful, paring cut to set in the eye socket. Refer to the photo for the cut.

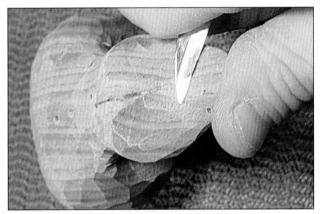

Photo 148 - **Trim down** the top of the beak.

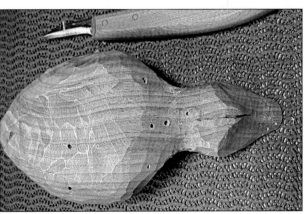

Photo 149- **When the eye socket cuts** are done and the beak is trimmed it should look like the photo.

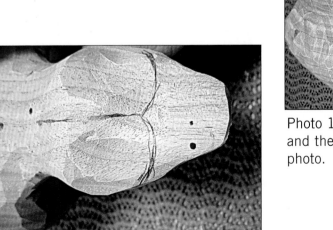

Photo 150 - **Draw in the top** of the beak as in the photo.

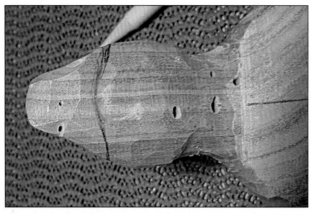

Photo 151 - **Draw in the bottom** as pictured.

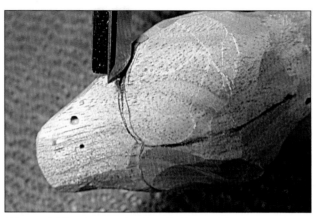

Photo 152- **Carve the beak line** with the v-tool or stop cut it with the knife.

Photo 153 - **Carefully trim** up to the cut on the top of the beak, leaving a sharp edge on the skull side of the cut.

Photo 154 - **Use the v-tool** to carve the line under the beak. Pare up to the line.

Photo 155 - **There should be** a clearly defined shadow when the line between the beak and the skull is completed. The next task is to create another line of shadow to separate the top and bottom of the beak.

Photo 156 - **V-tool,** or stop cut, a line to separate the two halves of the beak.

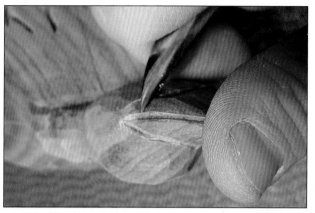

Photo 157- **Carefully trim** the bottom of the bill leaving the crisp edge on the top half of the beak.

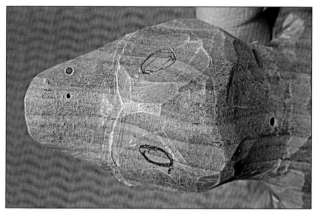

Photo 158 - **Draw oval shaped eyes** onto the duck's head in the center of the socket cuts made earlier. If you have a compass handy you can use it to mark the eyes. Put the point in one eye and use the pencil end to make a mark on the other. Put the point on the first mark and then mark the other eye.

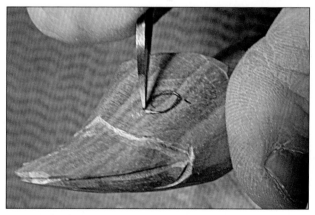

Photo 159 - **Put the knife tip** into the corner of the eye as pictured. Lay the knife into the wood along the pencil line.

Photo 160 - **Do the same** for the lower eyelid.

Photo 161 - **A levering cut** should pop out a single chip.

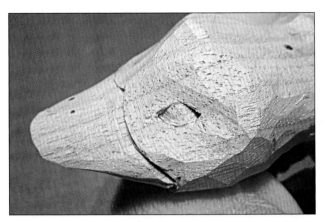

Photo 162 - **Repeat the process** for the back corner of the eye. With the knife or the v-tool, finish defining the upper and lower curves of the eyelid.

Photo 163 - **Don't forget** to do the other eye. Now that the details are complete, go back and carefully carve off the centerlines.

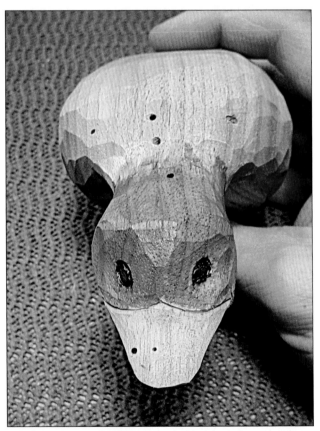

Photo 164 - **I decided to add** a little color. For a faded appearance, try water colors or very thin acrylics. Yellow for the beak and green for the head. With a very fine brush or a toothpick, paint the eye all black.

The painting is complete. Since the duck has been painted, a polyurethane finish is probably best. After that, it's ready for the shelf.

## Project Two: Little Bear

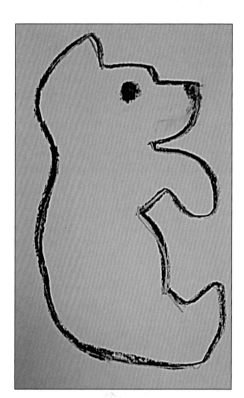

Photo 165 - **White cedar** 2 inches x 2 inches x 4 inches. I designed the pattern to hang over a book or a picture frame.

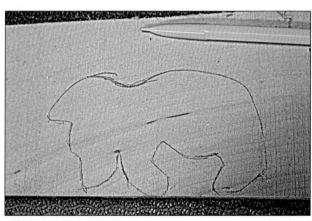

Photo 166 - **First, trace the pattern** onto the wood.

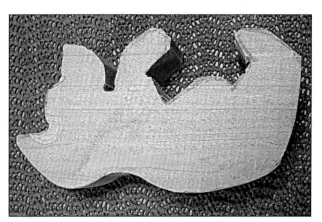

Photo 167 - **Band saw** the blank out being especially careful between the feet.

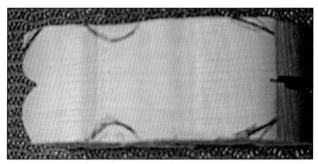

Photo 168 - **Mark off** the neck, ears, and backside as pictured.

Photo 169- **Draw a centerline** around the blank.

Photo 170 - **Mark the sides** of the snout midway between the centerline and the edge of the blank.

Photo 171 - **Mark the wood** to be removed between the paws. Also, mark the corners of the rear paws.

Photo 172 - **Begin carving** by paring off the outside of the ears.

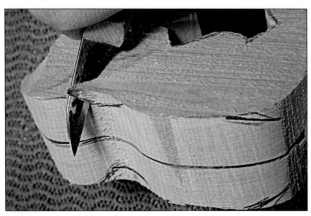

Photo 173 - **Begin to trim** the neck by paring from the head to the shoulder.

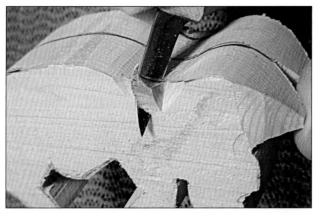

Photo 174 - **Continue** from the shoulder to the head.

Photo 175 - **Draw a line** for the neck.

Photo 176- **Stop cut** across the neck and pare up to the stop cut.

Photo 177 - **Pare down the back** and around the backside to the rear paws. Be certain to do both sides.

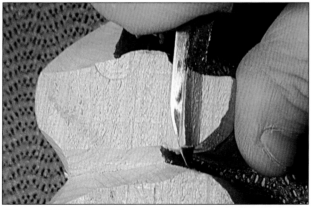

Photo 178 - **Pare from the cheek** to the end of the snout. Do both sides of the snout.

Photo 179 - **Removing the wood** from between the paws is very tricky. Gently pare from the paw to the center line.

Photo 180- **And lever cut** up to the centerline.

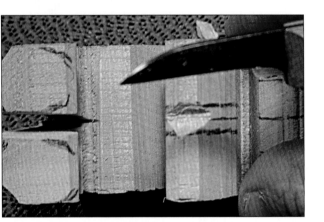

Photo 181 - **The first chip removed.**

Photo 182 - .......... **and again** pare and lever.

Photo 183 - **And again.**

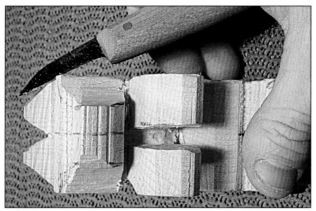

Photo 184 - **Caution and some slow work** will separate the paws.

Photo 185 - **Round the back** with more paring cuts. When complete there should be a series of strong cuts leaving the bear nice and round.

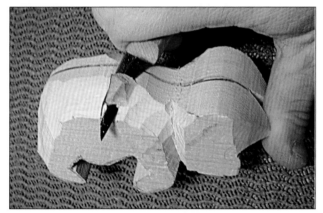

Photo 186 - **Pare up to the shoulder** from the belly.  Be certain to do both sides.

Photo 187 - **Pare the insides** of the legs. This is difficult work, similar to separating the front paws.

Photo 188 - **Use the knife** to trim the outsides of the legs.

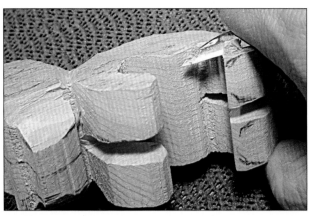

Photo 189 - **Carefully round** the paws by trimming off the corners.

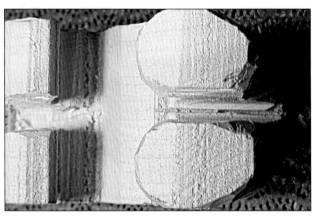

Photo 190 - **The paws** should look like the ones in the photo.

Photo 191 - **Carefully pare** the saw marks off the end of the rear paws.

Photo 192 - **Trim the edges** of the rear paws.

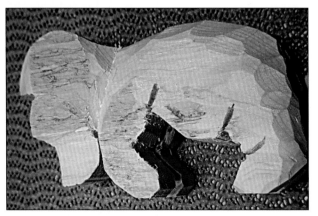

Photo 193 - **Mark where** all four legs meet the body as pictured, then mark where the rear paws meet the legs.

Photo 194 - **Stop cut** from the leg to the paw. Be careful not to break off the paw.

Photo 195 - **Lever up** to the first cut and remove the chip.

Photo 196 - **Pare** to the top of the leg.

Photo 197 - **Lever up** to the previous cut to remove the chip.

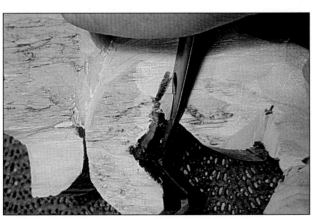

Photo 198 - **Lever cut** up to the front leg.

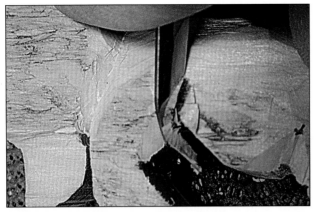

Photo 199 - **Pare down** to that cut.

Photo 200 - **Use the same technique** to the mark on the rear paw, and then do the same to the other side.

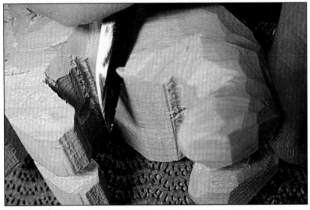

Photo 201 - **When those cuts** are completed, round the belly with paring cuts.

Photo 202 - **This work is very tricky**. The paws are cross-grained. Gently stop cut the paw at the wrist. Too firm a cut and the paw will come off.

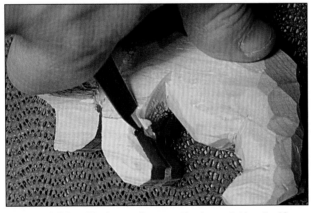

Photo 203 - **To be safe,** gently insert the knife tip as pictured and pare up to the shoulder.

Photo 204 - **Pare from the top** of the paw up to the shoulder.

Photo 205 - **Be very careful** because it will be easy to break off the paw at this point.

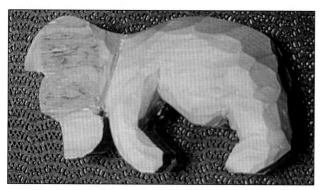

Photo 206 - **When the front legs** are complete, they should resemble this photo.

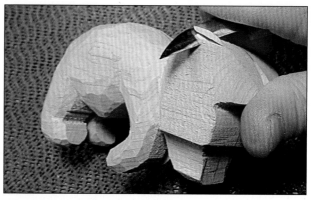

Photo 207 - **It is now time** to finish the head. Pare off the corner of the head.

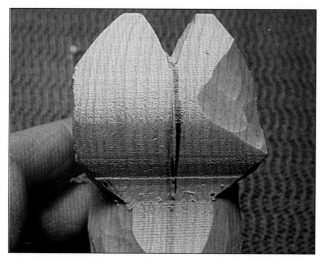

Photo 208 - **The head** should look like this after that cut.

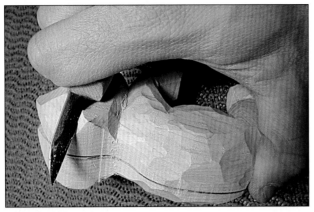

Photo 209 - **Pare off** the corners left by the earlier cuts.

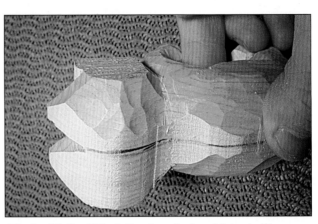

Photo 210 - **What the head** should look like.

Photo 211 - **Pare off** the corners of the ears. Try not to make the ears pointy. Leave some of the wood untouched.

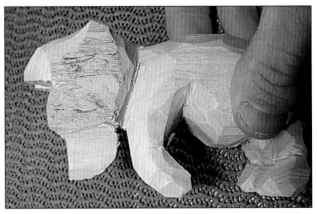

Photo 212 - **The ears** should look like those in the photo when complete.

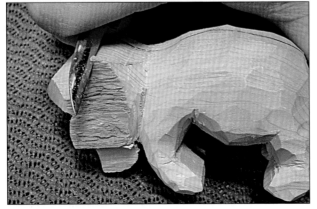

Photo 213 - **Pare off** the corner of the back of the head as earlier.

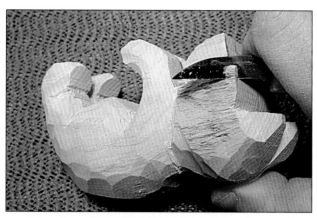

Photo 214 - **Pare off** the top corner of the head immediately in front of the ears.

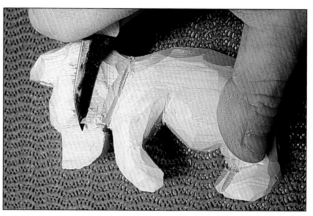

Photo 215 - **Pare down** some of the cheek to the neck.

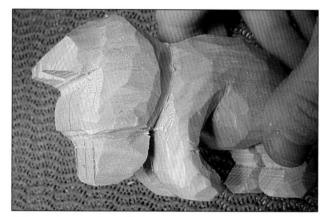

Photo 216 - **The face** should look like this when done.

Photo 217 - **Carve** the other side.

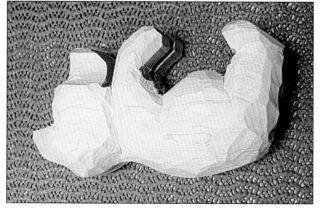

Photo 218 - **The head** roughed in.

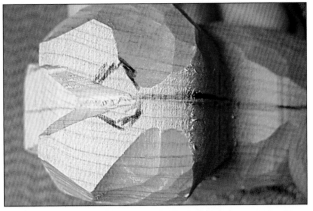

Photo 219 - **Mark the back** of the ears as in the photo.

Photo 220 - **Make a stop cut** into the back of the ear.

Photo 221 - **Lever** into that stop cut.

Photo 222 - **Repeat** the procedure for the other ear.

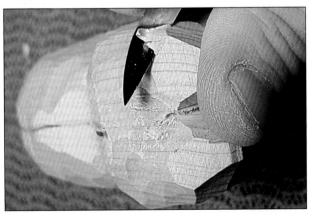

Photo 223 - **Gently round** the ear paring from the front to the back.

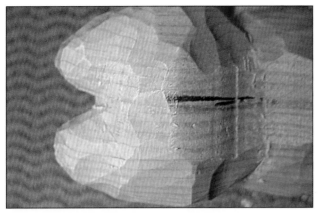

Photo 224 - **Both** completed ears.

Photo 225 - **Mark the insides** of the ears as in the photo.

Photo 226 - **Make a stop cut** into the ear. Deep at the base and shallower towards the top.

Photo 227 - **Make a stop cut** at the base of the ear from the mark to the outside.

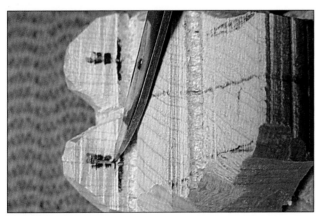

Photo 228 - **Make another** on the other side.

Photo 229 - **Insert the knife tip** into the first stop cut and pare out a chip. Reverse the carving and do the same to the other side of this ear.

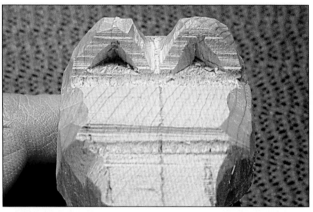

Photo 230 - **Once the ear is done**, make the stop cuts to the other ear and complete them.

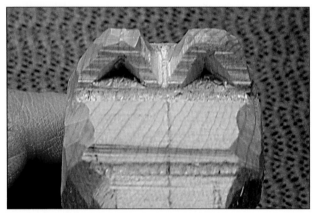

Photo 231 - **The ears hollowed out.**

Photo 232 - **Gently pare** around the outside of the ears.

Photo 233- **When both** are done, proceed to the snout.

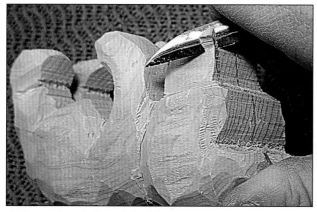

Photo 234 - **Pare** from the nose to the eye area.

Photo 235 - **This is what the snout** should look like with one angle of the snout pared. Pare the other side to match.

Photo 236 - **Pare off** the bottom edge of the snout. Both sides should be done.

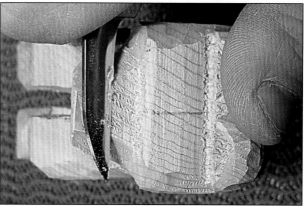

Photo 237 - **Pare the top** of the snout up to the eyebrows.

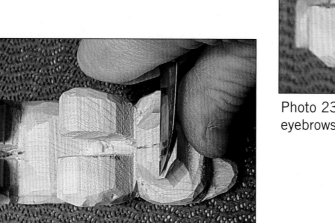

Photo 238 - **Gently trim off** the end of the nose. Pare off the saw marks from under the snout.

Photo 239 - **Round** the front paws and legs.

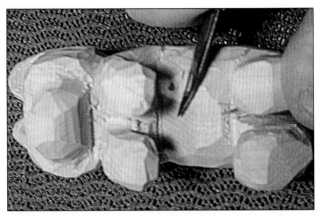

Photo 240 - **Trim the saw marks** off the belly and finish rounding. Go over the entire bear removing saw marks and pencil lines, as you go, round the bear.

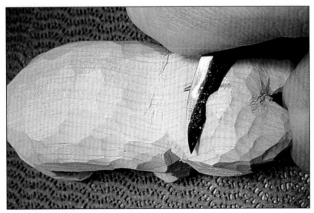

Photo 241 - **Don't forget** to round the head a little more.

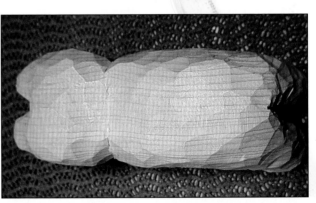

Photo 242 - **The final shaping** is now complete. The back of the bear should look like this photo.

Photo 243 - **Burn, paint, or carve** the bear. To carve or burn, mark the face as pictured. You can use a compass to make sure both eyes match.

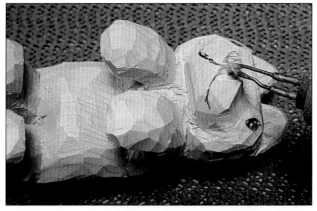

Photo 244 - **For the nose**, use the blade of the wood burner.

Photo 245 - **It should resemble** the photo.

Photo 246 - **Draw the mouth lines** in with the burner.

Photo 247 - **Lay the burner** into the corners of the eye.

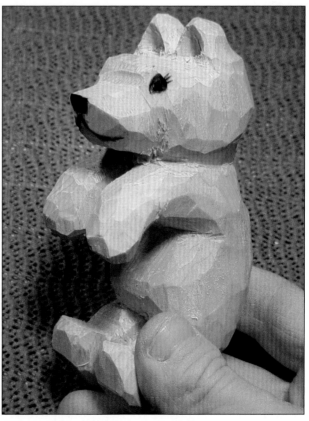

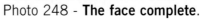
Photo 248 - **The face complete**.

## Project Three: Bearded Face

The last project is a stylized, bearded face. Once the steps for making this face are memorized, the options are endless. It's a great subject to carve onto a walking stick or a piece of found wood. (Photo 249)

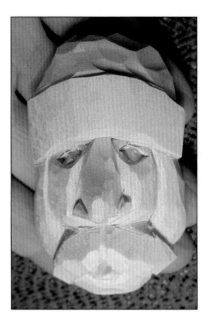

Photo 250 - **Select a piece** of basswood, pine or butternut that is 2 inches x 2 inches x 3 inches (left).

Photo 251 - **Use a square** or a ruler to draw a line from corner to corner.
Band saw the block in half as pictured. To do this safely, tilt the table of the band saw or build a jig to hold the block at the right angle.

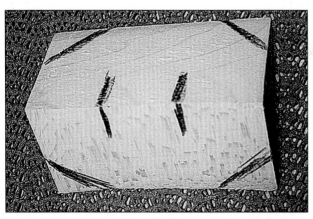

Photo 252 - **Mark the blank** as in the photo.

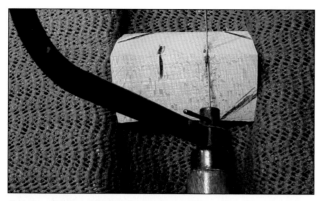

Photo 253 - **Make two stop cuts** with the knife or use a coping saw. Using a power tool to make these cuts is not a good idea.

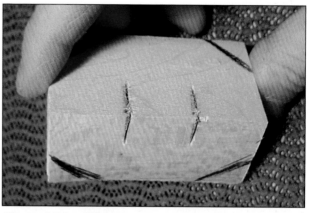

Photo 254 - **With the stop cuts complete**, the carving is ready to be started.

Photo 255 - **Cut off** all four marked corners as pictured.

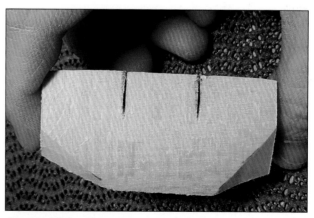

Photo 256 - **Be sure** to make the cuts consistent.

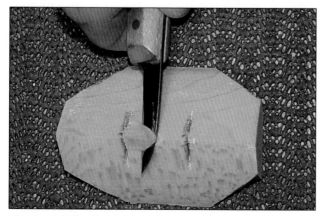

Photo 257 - **Decide which end** will be the top of the face. Use a lever cut to pare from the bottom cut down into the other stop cut.

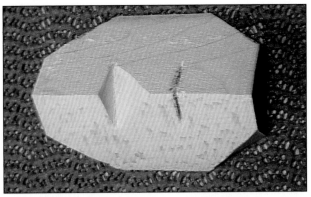

Photo 258 - **When the cut** is complete, it should resemble the photo.
Give the second stop cut the same treatment, cutting from the chin down to what will be the nose.

Photo 259 - **Make a levering cut** from the area over the eye up to the eyebrow and remove the chip with a stop cut.

Photo 260 - **One side complete.**

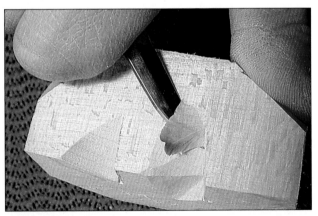

Photo 261 - **Turn the blank** around and repeat but this time use a paring cut. Remove the chip with a stop cut.

Photo 262 - **The eyebrow** is now roughed in.

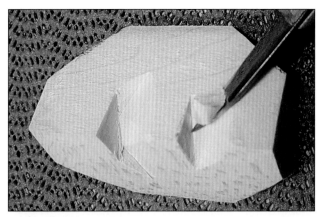

Photo 263 - **Repeat the process** under the nose to define the lip and moustache with a levering cut.

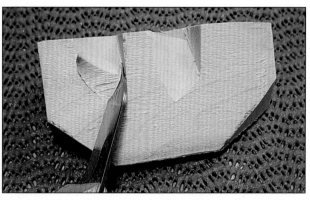

Photo 264 - **On the opposite side** make another stop cut.

Photo 265 - **Reverse the blank** and start with another paring cut and remove the chip with another stop cut.

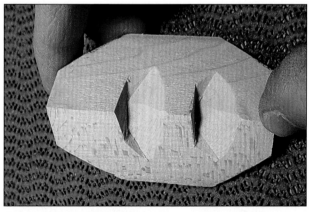

Photo 266 - **The face** should resemble the photo. For the moment the eyebrow and nose areas should be identical.

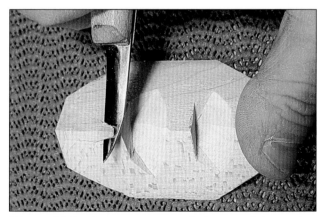

Photo 267 - **Remove** some of the wood from the eyebrow to the top of the head.

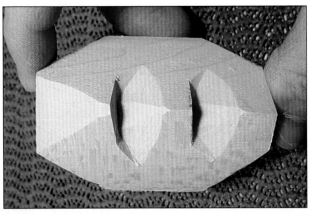

Photo 268 - **This will lower** the top of the forehead. Do the same to the area beneath the nose.

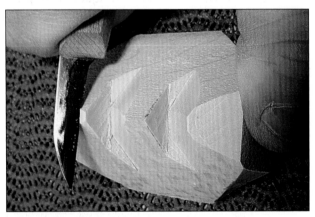

Photo 270 - **Make an angled stop cut** into the eyebrow. Now we are ready to mark up the blank again.

Photo 272 - **There is a small** triangular opening for the mouth. Make a stop cut along each side of the moustache.

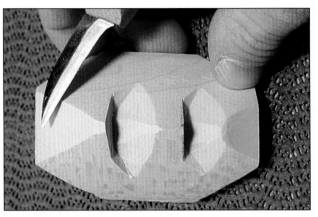

Photo 269 - **It should resemble the photo.**

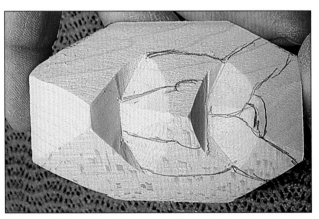

Photo 271 - **Mark the blank** as pictured. Mark the sides of the nose, the moustache, the lips and the sides of the face.

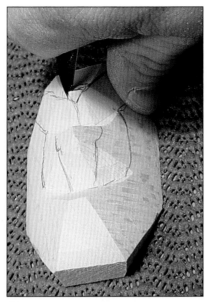

Photo 273 - **With only** the point of the blade, use a paring cut to pop out the chip.

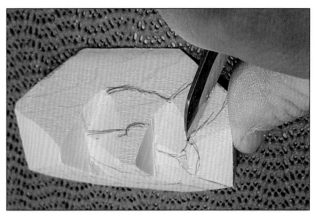

Photo 274 - **Use the same techniques** into the corner of the mouth under the lip. Stop cut along the moustache.

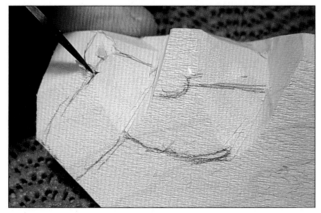

Photo 275 - **Make another** stop cut along the lip.

Photo 276 - **Lever out** the chip. Repeat the process on the other side, make a stop cut straight under the lip.

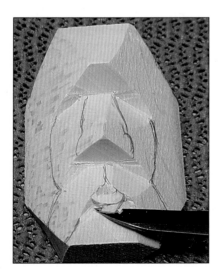

Photo 277 - **Pare up** to the stop cut.

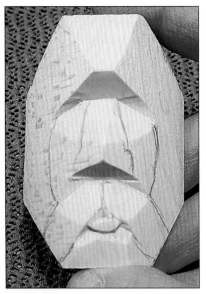

Photo 278 - **The mouth** should look like this.

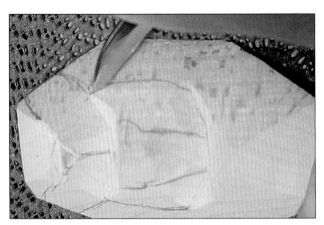

Photo 279 - **Stop cut** into the lower corner of the face.

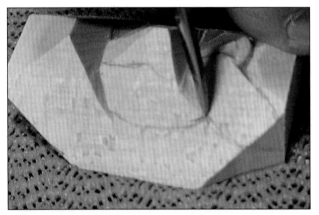

Photo 280 - **Stop cut** the other side and pop out the chip.

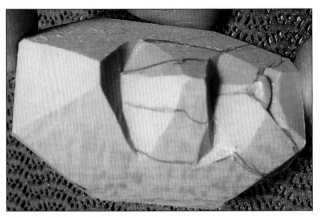

Photo 281 - **One side done.**

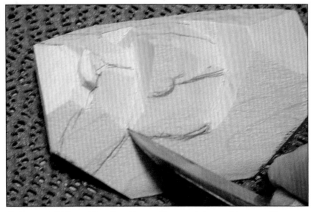

Photo 282 - **Begin** the other side with another stop cut.

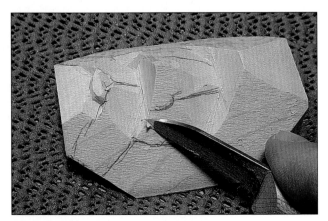

Photo 283 - **Add** a second stop cut.

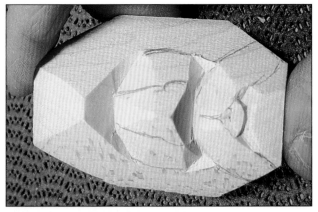

Photo 284 - **Both sides cut in.**

Photo 285 - **Define the sides** of the face by stop cutting along the line.

Photo 286 - **Pare out** a thin sliver.

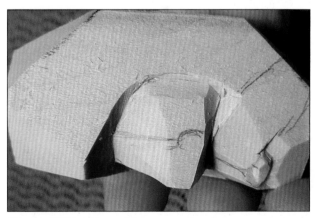

Photo 287 - **One side now complete.**

Photo 288 - **All of the following cuts** can be made with the knife, however a v-tool is a better choice if available.

Photo 289 - **Use the v-tool** to carve in the lines of the moustache.

Photo 290 - **Next**, work on the nose.

Photo 291 - **Stop cut** into the corner of the eye.

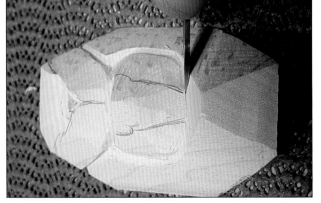

Photo 292 - **Stop cut** along the brow.

Photo 293 - **Remove the chip** to set in the corner of the eye.

Photo 294 - **Repeat** on the other side.

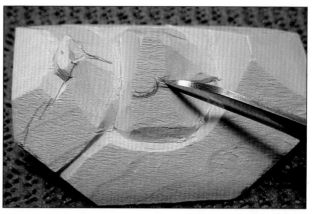

Photo 295 - **The corner** of the nostril is stop cut into the nose.

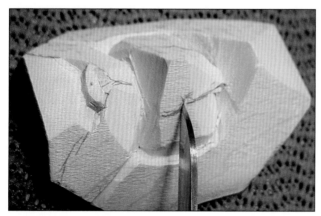

Photo 296 - **Make another** stop cut over the nostril.

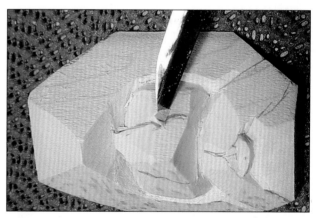

Photo 297 - **Lever cut** to remove the chip.

Photo 298 - **Make sure** to repeat on the other side.

Photo 299 - **Run the v-tool** up the side of the nose into the corner of the eye. Do both sides of the nose.

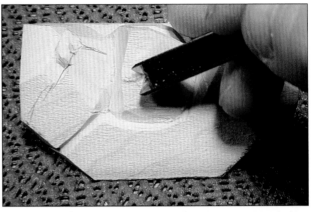

Photo 300 - **Using a v-tool** or with the knife, carve around the nostril line.

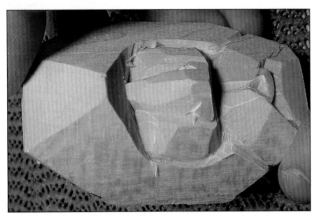

Photo 301 - **Both sides** of the nose are done.

Photo 302 - **Use a stop cut** to remove the corners of the nose.

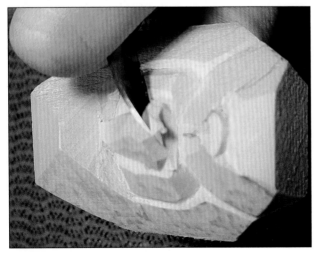

Photo 303 - **Pare under** the nose at a bit of an angle.

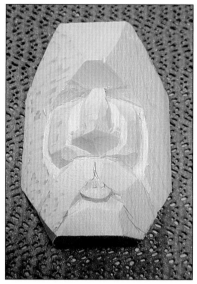

Photo 304 - **The nose** is roughed in.

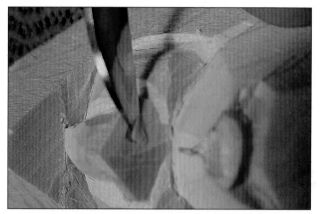

Photo 305 - **Force the blade** into the wood under the nose to open the nostril. Do both sides.

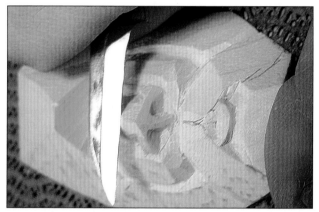

Photo 306 - **Trim off** the end of the nose. This finishes the nose.

Photo 307 - **Use the v-tool** or knife to separate the halves of the moustache.

Photo 308 - **Deepen** the moustache a bit.

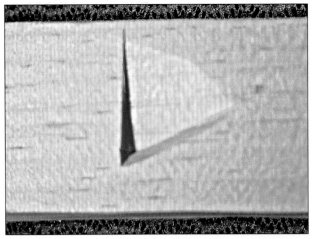

Photo 309 - **It is now time** to do the eyes. It's a good idea to obtain a bit of scrap wood to get the hang of it. Make two stop cuts and a paring cut to make the scrap resemble the eye socket of the carving.

Photo 310 - **Draw a football** eye shape. Make a stop cut into the corner of the eye.

Photo 311 - **Make** the second stop cut.

Photo 312 - **Lever out** the chip.

Photo 313 - **Repeat the process** and stop cut one side.

Photo 314 - **Stop cut** the other side.

Photo 315 - **Pop out** the chip.

Photo 316 - **Use the knife** to trim under the eyelid.

Photo 317 - **Repeat** for the bottom eyelid.

Photo 318 - **Super!** Now for the real thing.

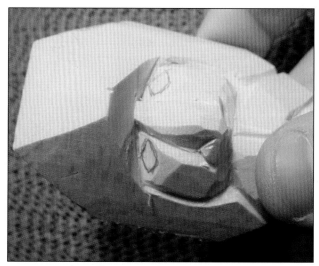

Photo 319 - **Mark the eyes.**

Photo 320 - **The first stop cut.**

Photo 321 - **The second stop cut.** Remove the chip.

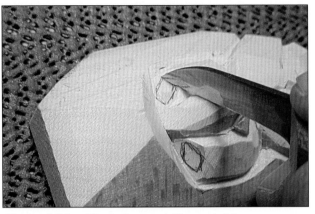

Photo 322 - **First stop cut** the outside corner.

Photo 323 - **The second stop cut.** Remove the chip.

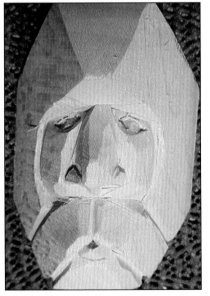

Photo 324 - **The eyes are done.**

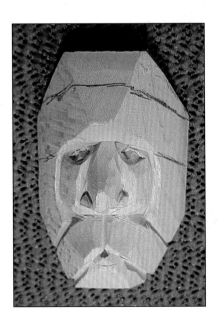

Photo 325 - **We'll finish this** as a mountain man with a coonskin cap. Mark the brim of the cap.

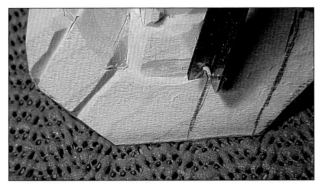

Photo 326 - **V-tool** the bottom of the brim.

Photo 327 - **Also** the top of the brim.

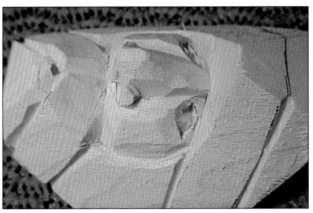

Photo 328 - **The brim** roughed in.

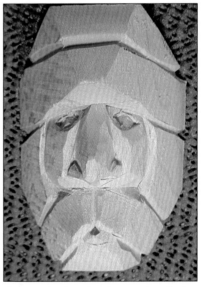

Photo 329 - **At the ends** of the v-tooled lines cut out a chip to separate the hat and hair.

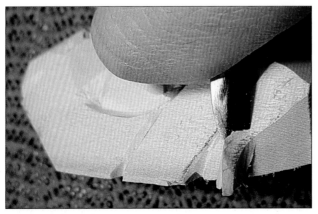

Photo 330 - **Pare** the hat down.

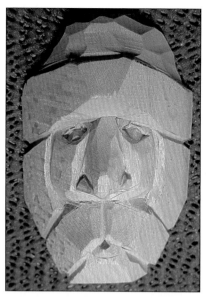

Photo 331 - **The hat** should resemble this photo.

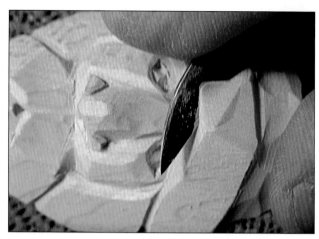

Photo 332 - **Round** the brim.

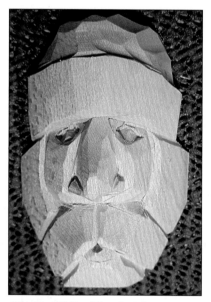

Photo 333 - **The hat** is complete.

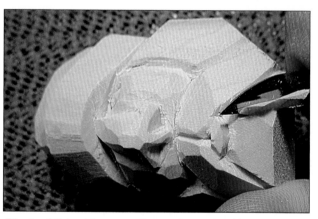

Photo 334 - **Deepen the cuts** under the moustache.

Photo 335 - **The chin complete.**

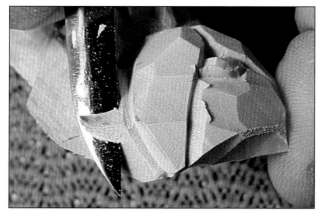

Photo 336 - **Trim up** to the beard.

Photo 337 - **It should** resemble the photo.

Photo 338 - **Trim the hair.**

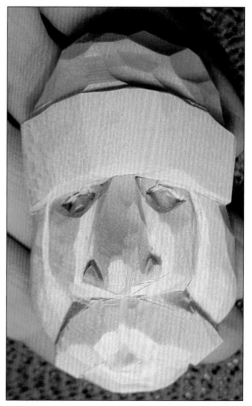

Photo 339 - **The face is complete.**

# A few ideas and resources

This book is intended to be a starting point. In this section, I've included some Internet resource I found to be useful. I have no affiliation with any of the resources except for the New England Wood Carvers and the National Wood Carvers Association. I am a member of both organizations and a past president of NEWC. I highly recommend both organizations as priceless sources of information and friends.

## Some random ideas

I have found that tackle boxes, especially some of the sectioned ones, are excellent for carrying knives and palm tools. The plastic prevents damage to the blades and keeps everything safe. Shallow plastic drawers from office supply stores are useful for storing full sized tools. They frequently come with wheels that make them more portable.

Every woodcarving area should have a first aid kit. At a minimum this should include sterile dressings and bandages of various sizes as well as antiseptic. The quicker the cut is cleaned and dressed, the quicker you can get back to carving.

You can turn digital pictures into line drawings by using the "Edge Detection" filters of many popular graphics editing tools.

## Childhood development resources

Parents Action for Children
http://www.iamyourchild.org/

Child Development & Parenting Information
http://www.cdipage.com/

Child Development resources
http://www.cdr.org/

Attention Deficit Disorder
http://www.add.org/

Bipolar Disorder
http://www.bpkids.org/

Autism
http://www.autism-pdd.net/

## Woodcarving resources

The National Wood Carvers Association
http://www.chipchats.org/
The National Wood Carvers Association is dedicated to the interests of amateur and professional carvers and whittlers. The NWCA is probably best known for its publication, **Chip Chats**. Six times a year, NWCA members receive **Chip Chats,** a magazine full of useful information for, and great carvings by, wood carvers. **Chip Chats** ranges in length from 148 to 164 pages. In addition, there are no paid advertisements so the pages are taken up only by great articles and photographs of carvings.

New England Wood Carvers
http://www.newc.org/
The New England Woodcarvers were organized in 1965. Their mission is to promote and encourage woodcarving, wood sculpture, and whittling as art forms and to stimulate and educate the community in these art forms. Thirty years later, in October of 1995, the New England Woodcarvers became the first woodcarving organization on the World Wide Web.

New England Woodcarvers, Inc.
P.O. Box 561
Lexington, MA 02420-0005

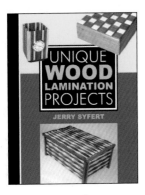
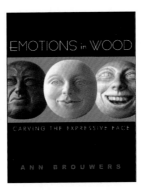
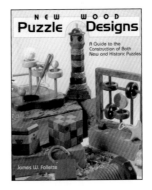

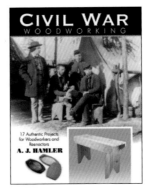

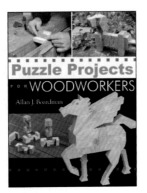